ISBN 0-7935-3652-9

7777 W. BLUEMOUND RD. P.O. BOX 13819 MILWAUKEE, WI 53213

EASY ADULT Piano

COUNTRY HITS

BASICS

Here are some things which will make your piano playing easier and more fun.

NOTES THAT NAME THEMSELVES

Easy Adult Piano music is written on a double staff. The upper staff is the **treble** (𝄞) staff and contains the melody usually played by your right hand. The lower **bass** (𝄢) staff contains the accompaniment part and is played by your left hand.

The **lower bass staff** in Easy Adult Piano has a unique feature to help make your playing easier. There are letters in the notes. If you're not used to reading bass notes, the letters will help you learn faster and play better.

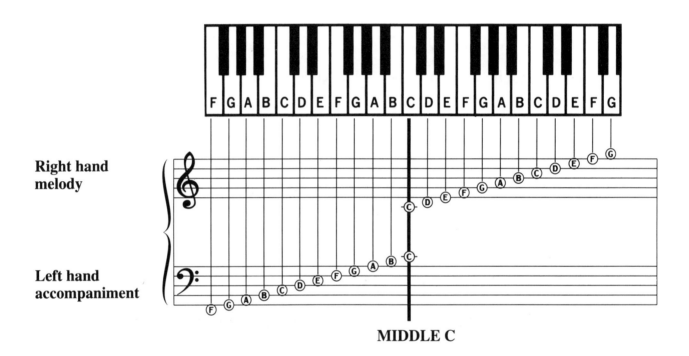

NOTE VALUES

In music, time is measured in **beats**. The illustration below shows the types of notes you'll play and how many beats each type receives.

Rests are shown in the lower part of the illustration, along with the number of beats each type receives. A **rest** indicates a period of silence — when you don't play. Rests are still counted, however.

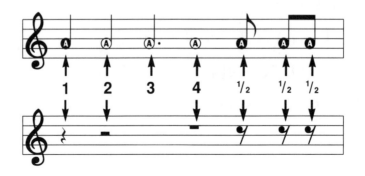

PLAYING THE BLACK KEYS

To make your playing easier, **sharps** (♯) or **flats** (♭) are placed in front of all notes to be played on black keys.

A flat (♭) before a note lowers the pitch of the note to the next key to the left.

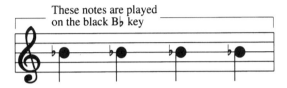

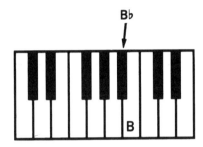

A sharp (♯) before a note raises the pitch of the note to the next key to the right.

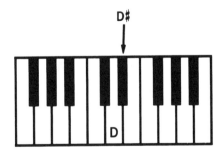

CHORD SYMBOLS

Small **chord symbols** appear above your music.

If you know something about harmony, you can use the chord symbols as a guide to create your own pianistic "touches" for each arrangement.

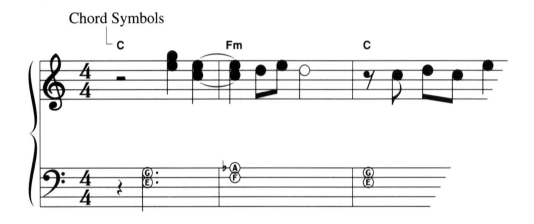

FINGERING

Small numbers appear near some of the notes. These are finger numbers and they'll help you play more smoothly. They correspond to your fingers as shown. If you use the finger numbers to play the indicated notes, you'll find playing a lot easier. If, while you're playing, you find a fingering style you like better, use it.

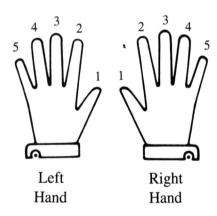

Left
Hand

Right
Hand

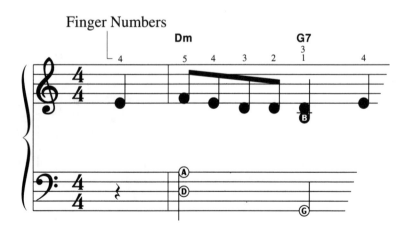

PEDALING SYMBOLS

Occasionally, use of the **sustain pedal** is indicated by these symbols. Press, hold, and release the pedal as indicated in the illustration below.

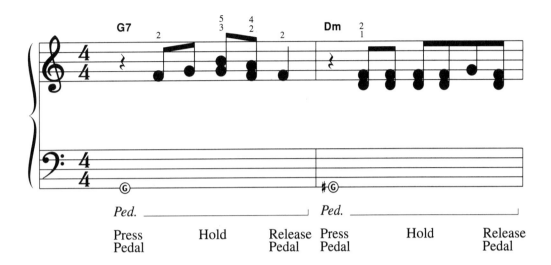

| Press Pedal | Hold | Release Pedal | Press Pedal | Hold | Release Pedal |

8va

This is an **octave** sign. It appears above or below certain groups of notes to indicate they should be played an octave (8 letter names) higher than written. **8va basso** indicates notes which are to be played an octave lower than written.

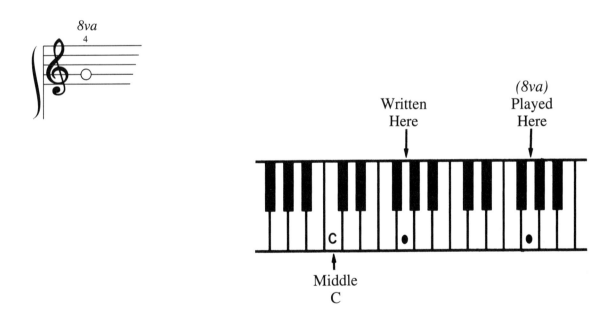

TEMPO AND RHYTHM

A suggested **tempo** usually appears at the beginning of each Easy Adult Piano arrangement. Use this as a guide to how fast or slow you should be playing.

Along with the tempo, in most cases, is a **rhythm** name (SWING, WALTZ, etc.) This is also a guide to the rhythmic "feel" the arrangement should have.

ACHY BREAKY HEART
(a.k.a. DON'T TELL MY HEART)

Words and Music by
DON VON TRESS

Moderate, WITH A STEADY BEAT

You can tell the world you nev - er was my girl. __
You can tell your ma I moved to Ark - an - sas. __

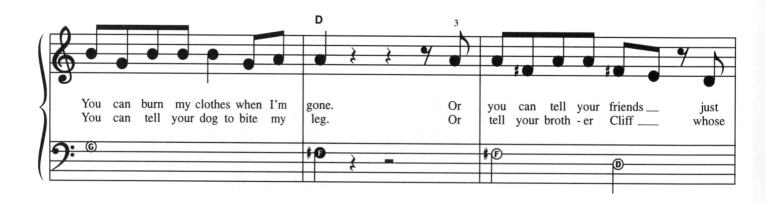

You can burn my clothes when I'm gone. Or you can tell your friends __ just
You can tell your dog to bite my leg. Or tell your broth - er Cliff __ whose

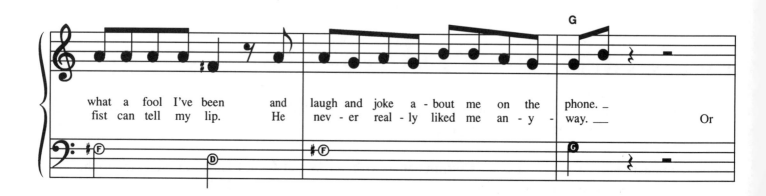

what a fool I've been and laugh and joke a - bout me on the phone. __
fist can tell my lip. He nev - er real - ly liked me an - y - way. __ Or

You can tell my arms go back __ to the farm. ____ You can tell my feet to hit the
tell your Aunt Lou -ise. Tell an - y - thing you please. __ My - self al - read - y knows I'm not o -

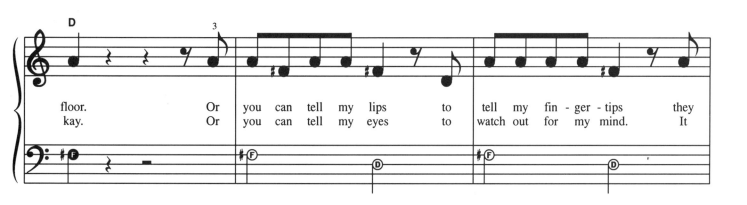

floor. Or you can tell my lips to tell my fin - ger - tips they
kay. Or you can tell my eyes to watch out for my mind. It

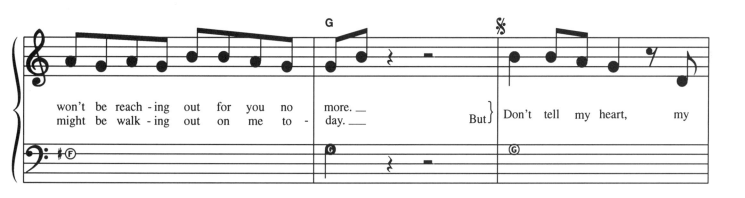

won't be reach - ing out for you no more. __ But } Don't tell my heart, my
might be walk - ing out on me to - day. __

ach - y break - y heart. __ I just don't think he'd un - der - stand. And

To Coda ⊕

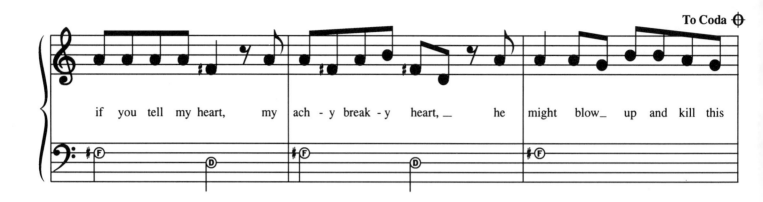

if you tell my heart, my ach - y break - y heart, ___ he might blow___ up and kill this

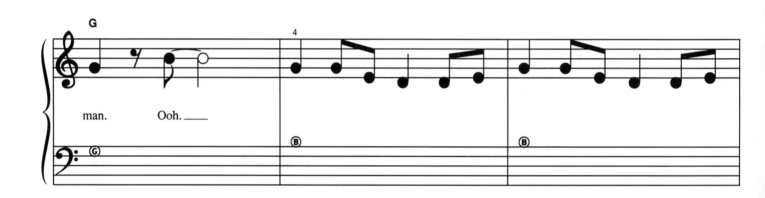

man. Ooh. ___

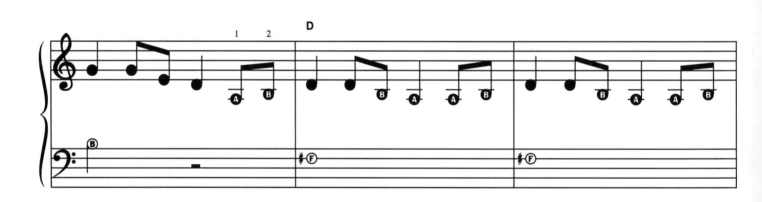

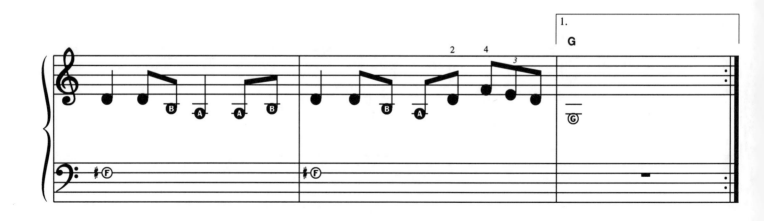

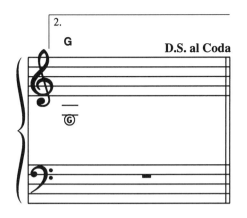

man. Don't tell my heart, my

ach - y break - y heart. __ I just don't think he'd un - der - stand. And

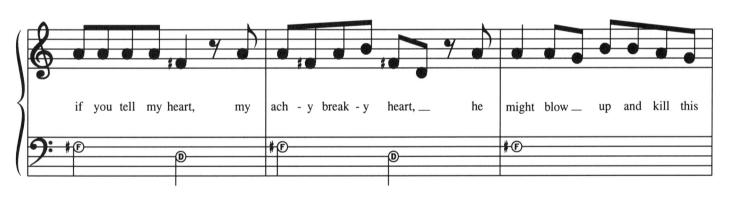

if you tell my heart, my ach - y break - y heart, __ he might blow __ up and kill this

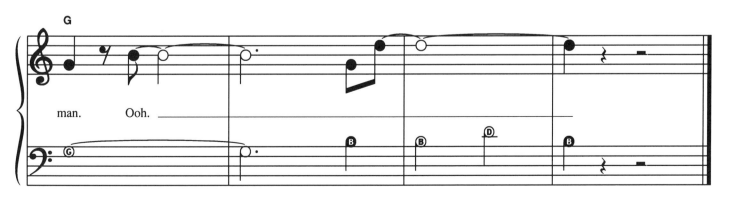

man. Ooh. _____

BOOT SCOOTIN' BOOGIE

Words and Music by
RONNIE DUNN

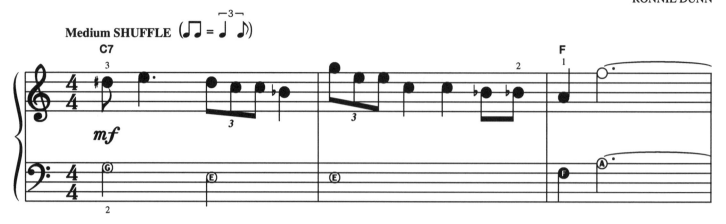

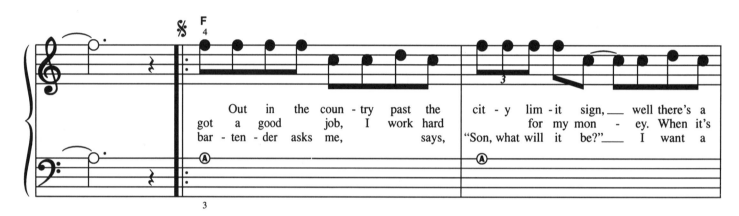

Out in the coun - try past the
got a good job, I work hard
bar - ten - der asks me, says,

cit - y lim - it sign, ___ well there's a
for my mon - ey. When it's
"Son, what will it be?" ___ I want a

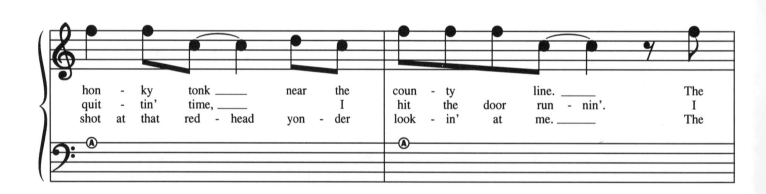

hon - ky tonk ___ near the
quit - tin' time, ___ I
shot at that red - head yon - der

coun - ty line. ___ The
hit the door run - nin'. I
look - in' at me. ___ The

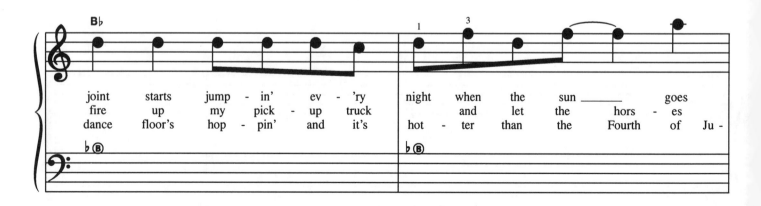

joint starts jump - in' ev - 'ry
fire up my pick - up truck
dance floor's hop - pin' and it's

night when the sun ___ goes
and let the hors - es
hot - ter than the Fourth of Ju -

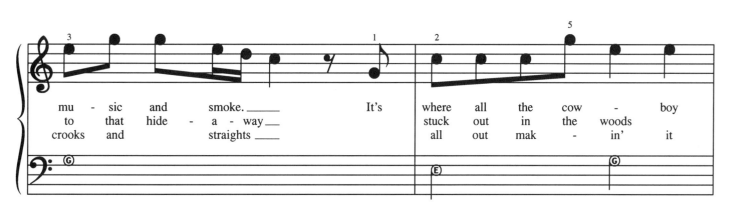

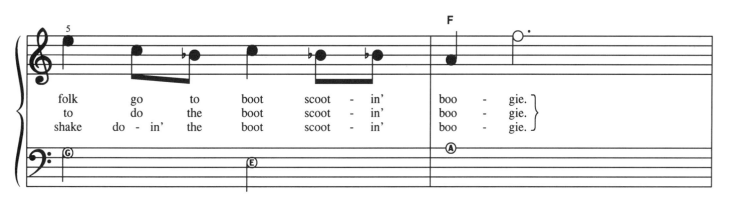

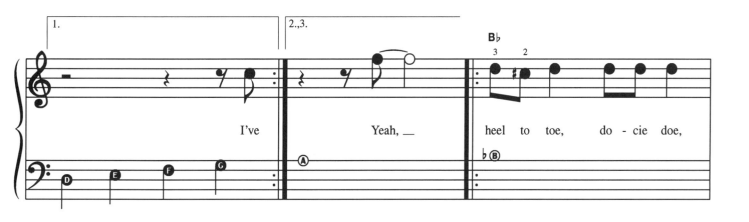

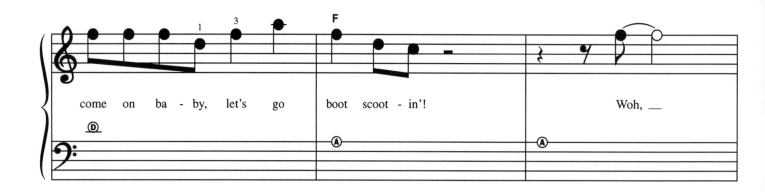

come on ba - by, let's go boot scoot - in'! Woh, ___

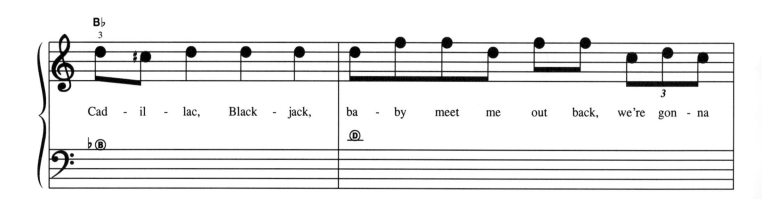

Cad - il - lac, Black - jack, ba - by meet me out back, we're gon - na

boo - gie. Oh, ___ get down, turn a - round, ___

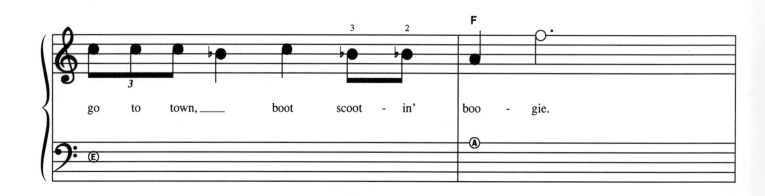

go to town, ___ boot scoot - in' boo - gie.

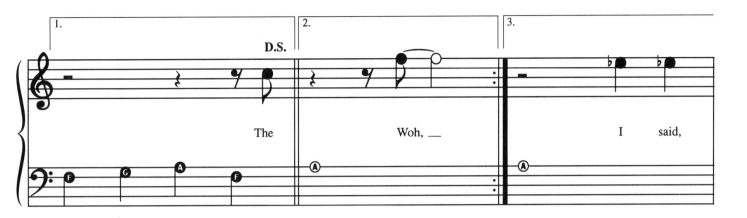

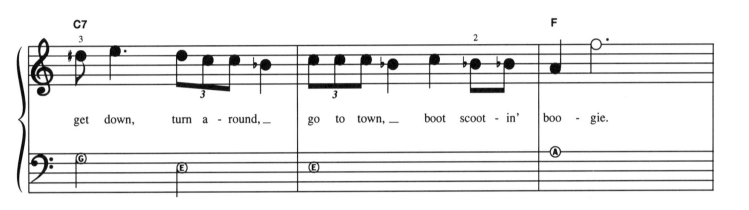

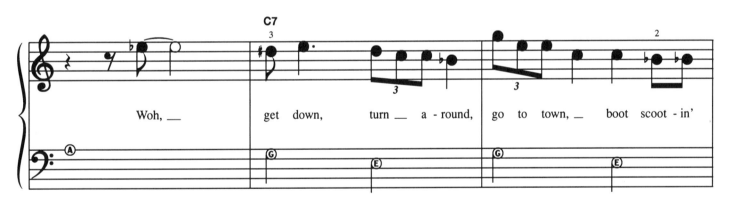

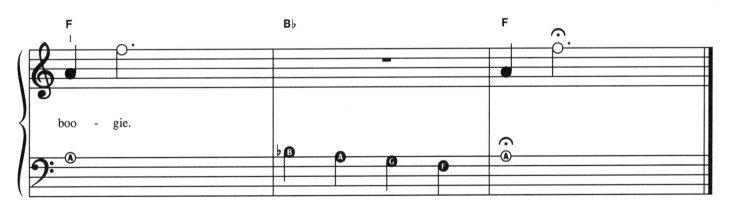

CHATTAHOOCHEE

Words and Music by JIM McBRIDE
and ALAN JACKSON

Bright COUNTRY 2-STEP

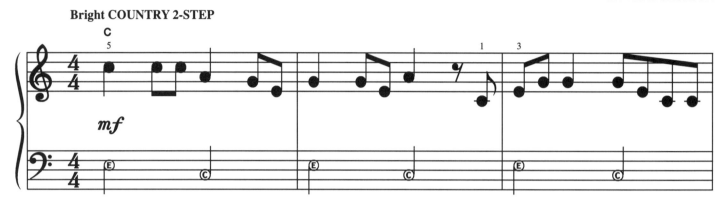

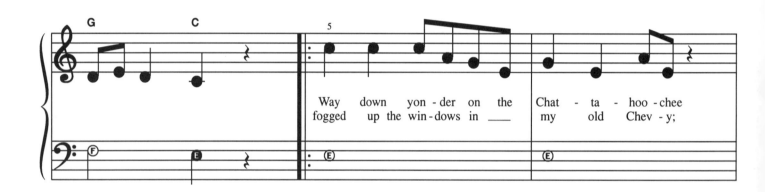

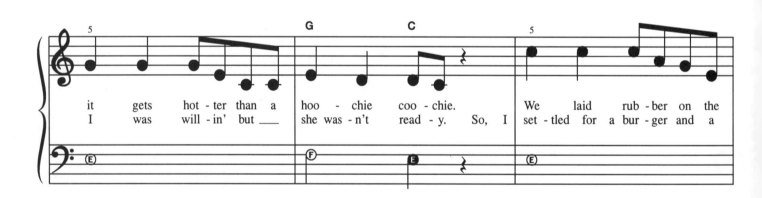

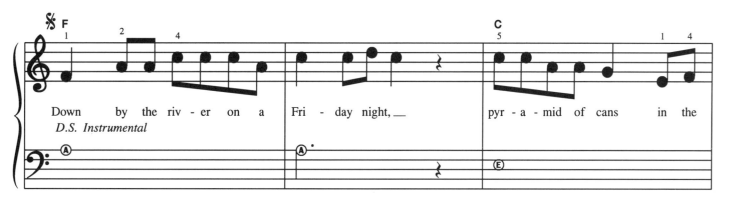

Down by the riv-er on a Fri - day night, pyr - a - mid of cans in the

D.S. Instrumental

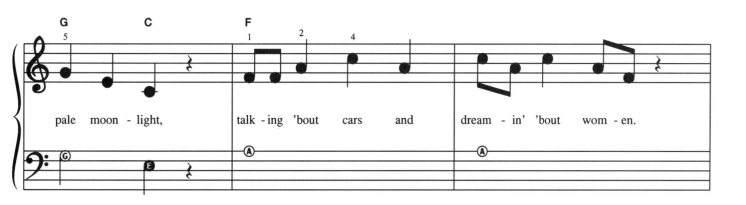

pale moon - light, talk -ing 'bout cars and dream - in' 'bout wom - en.

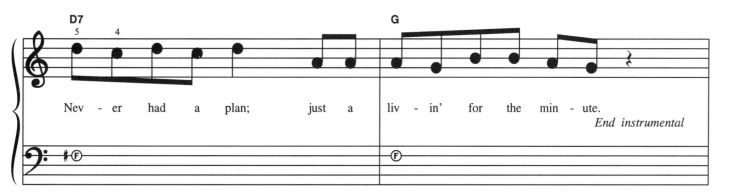

Nev - er had a plan; just a liv - in' for the min - ute.

End instrumental

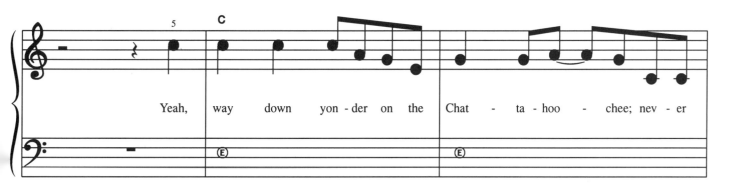

Yeah, way down yon -der on the Chat - ta - hoo - chee; nev - er

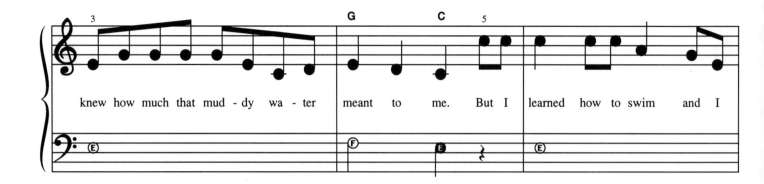

knew how much that mud - dy wa - ter meant to me. But I learned how to swim and I

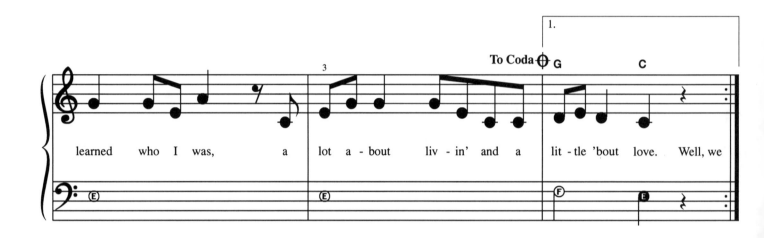

learned who I was, a lot a - bout liv - in' and a lit - tle 'bout love. Well, we

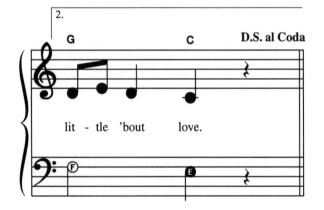

lit - tle 'bout love.

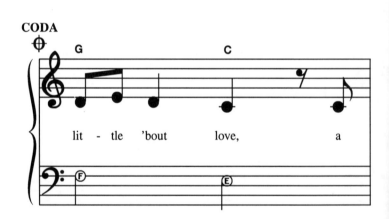

lit - tle 'bout love, a

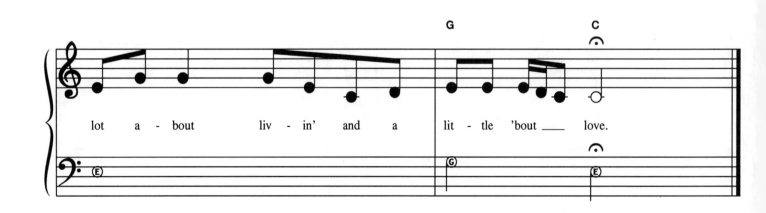

lot a - bout liv - in' and a lit - tle 'bout _____ love.

COULD I HAVE THIS DANCE

Words and Music by WAYLAND HOLYFIELD
and BOB HOUSE

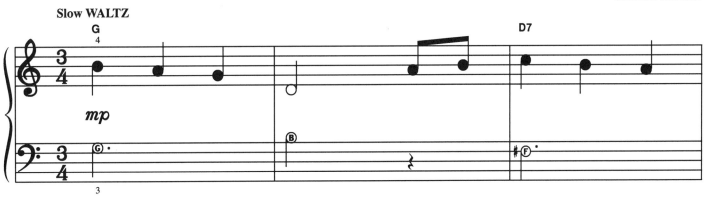

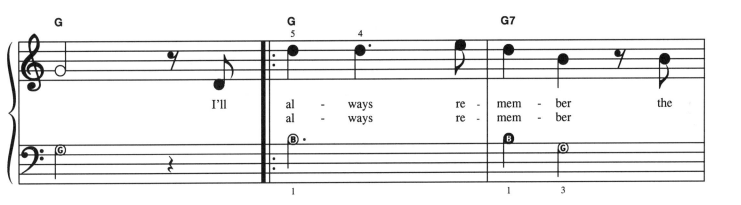

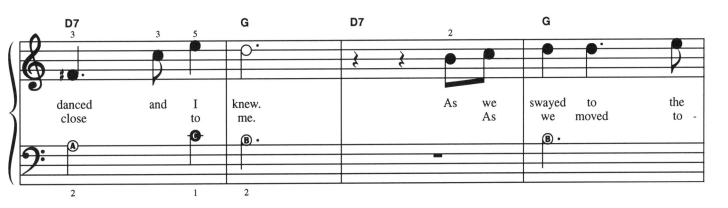

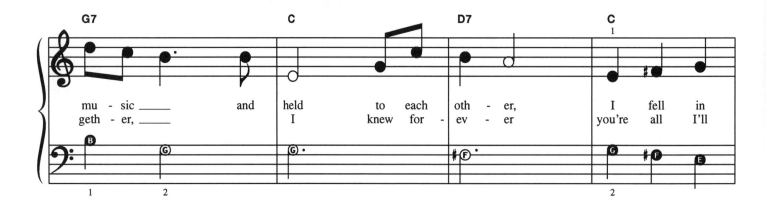

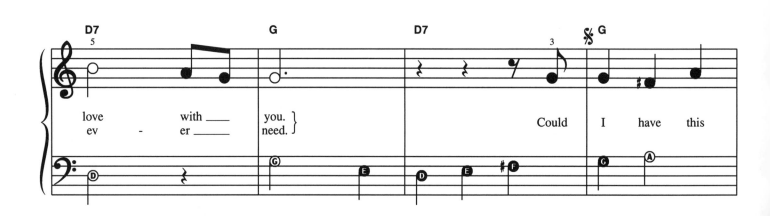

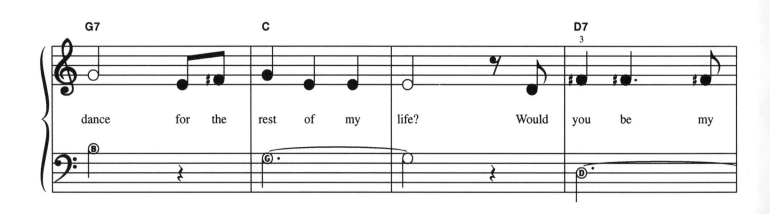

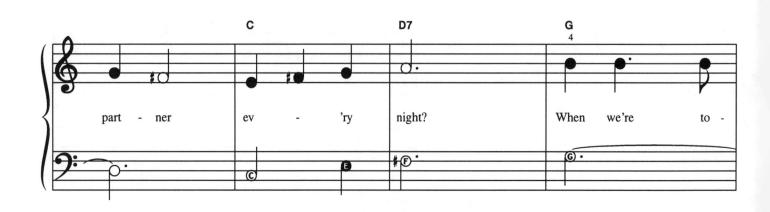

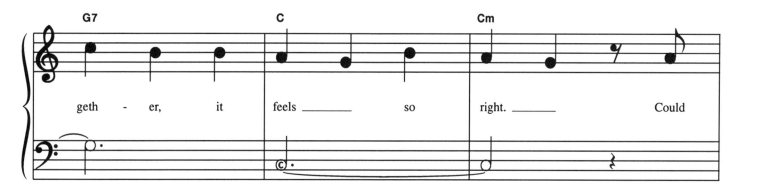

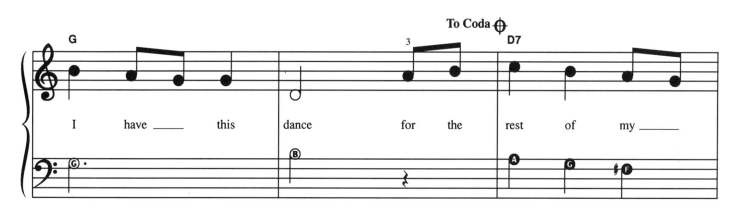

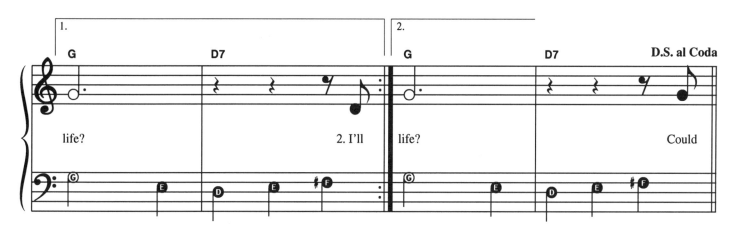

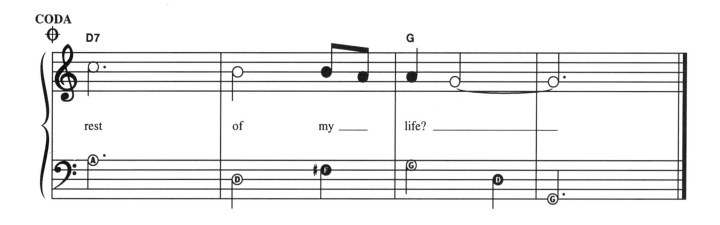

CRAZY

Words and Music by
WILLIE NELSON

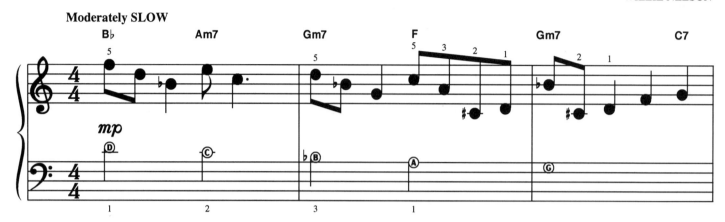

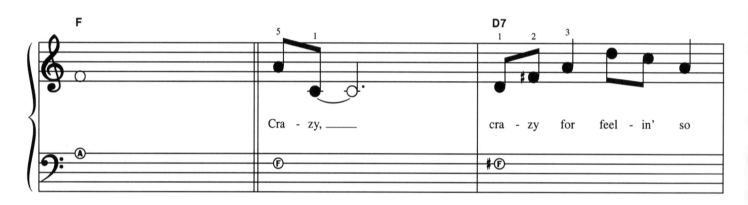

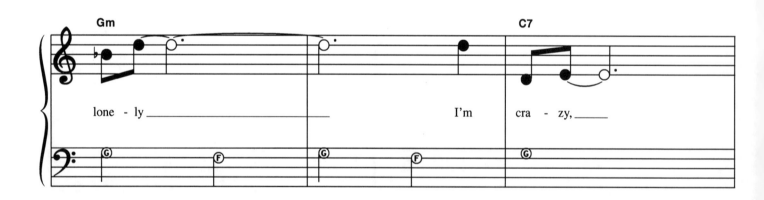

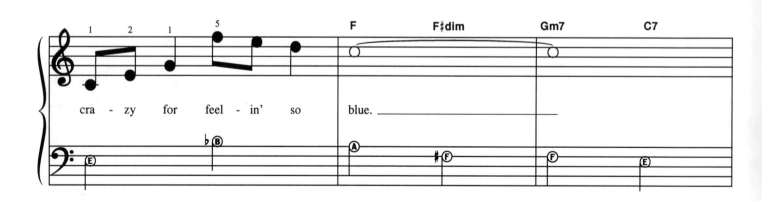

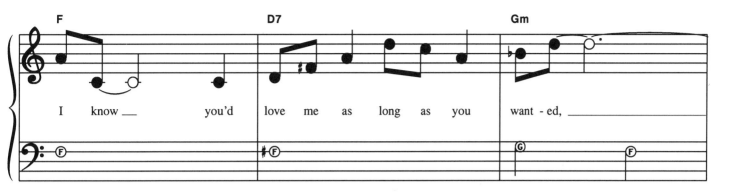

I know ____ you'd love me as long as you want - ed, _____

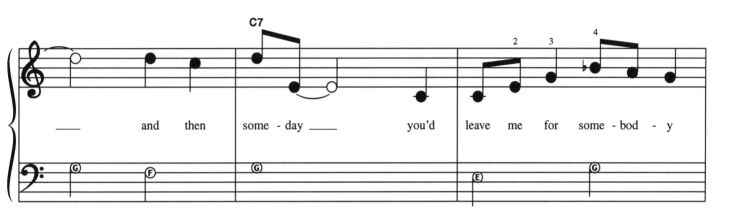

____ and then some - day ____ you'd leave me for some - bod - y

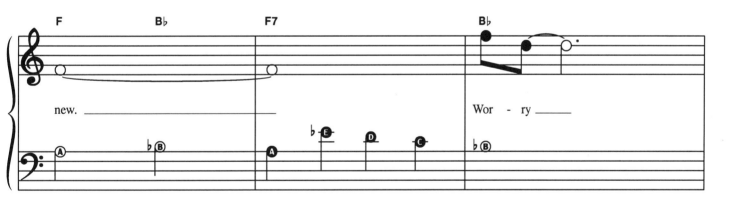

new. _____ Wor - ry _____

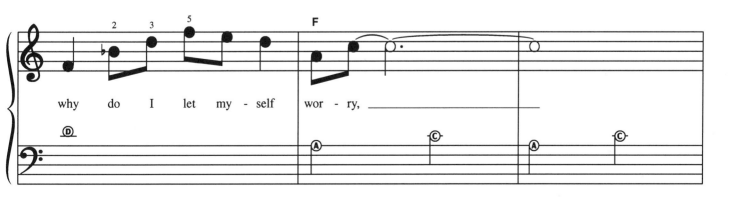

why do I let my - self wor - ry, _____

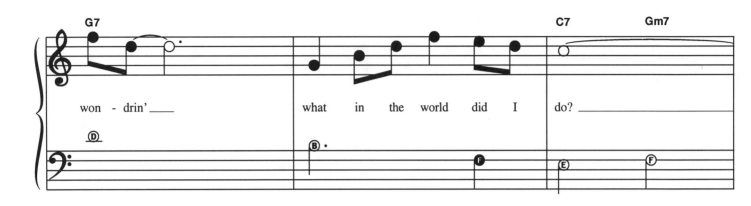

won - drin' _____ what in the world did I do? _____

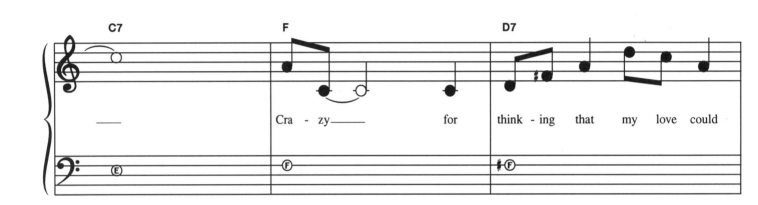

_____ Cra - zy _____ for think - ing that my love could

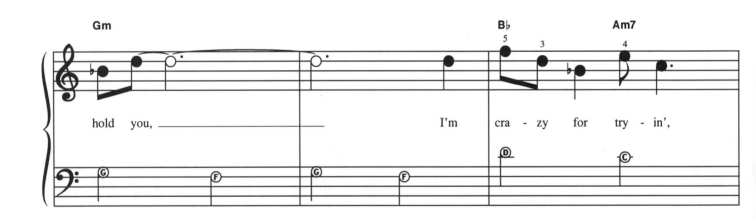

hold you, _____ I'm cra - zy for try - in',

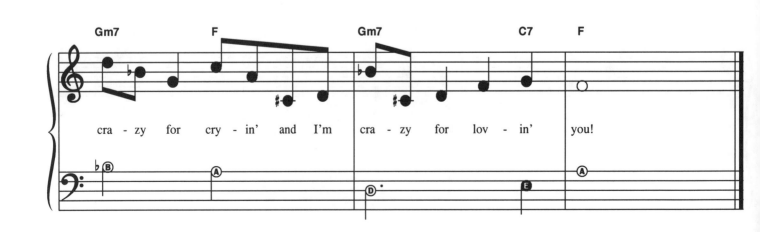

cra - zy for cry - in' and I'm cra - zy for lov - in' you!

THE DANCE

Words and Music by
TONY ARATA

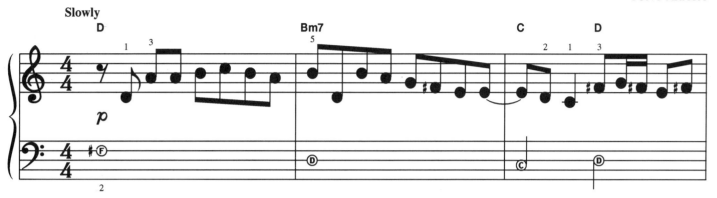

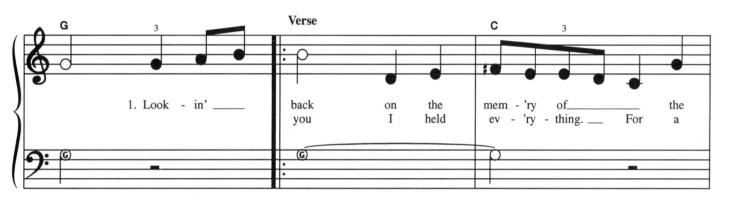

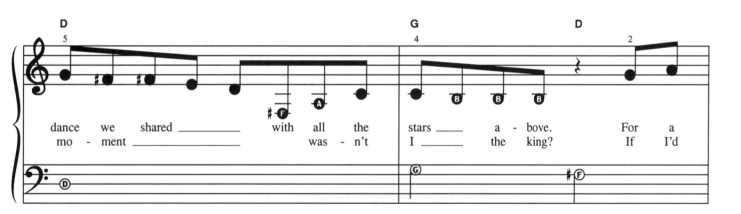

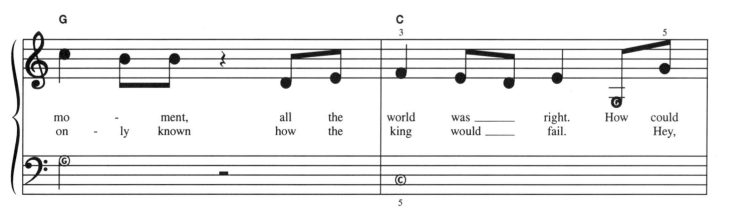

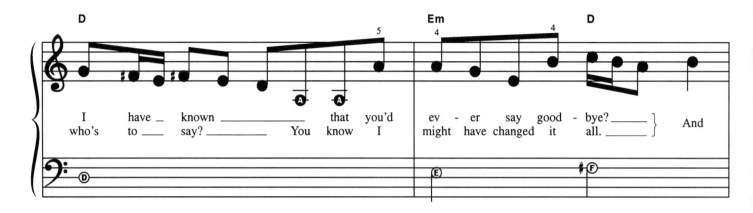

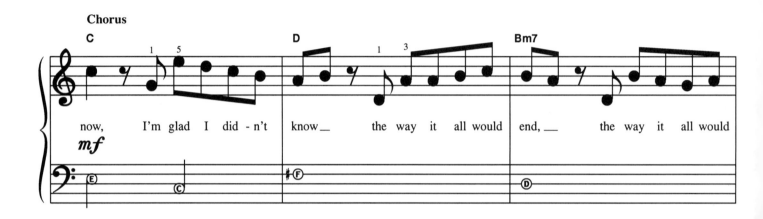

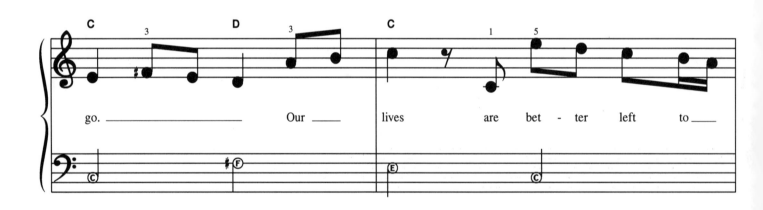

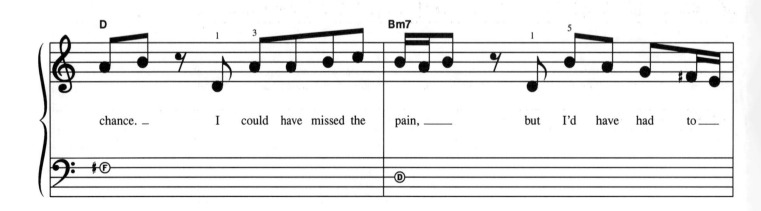

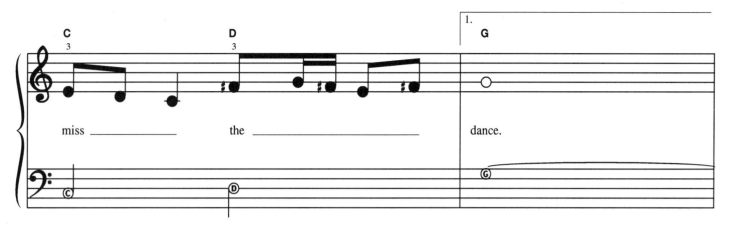

miss _____ the _____ dance.

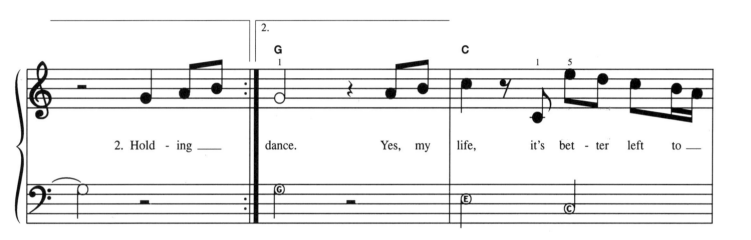

2. Hold - ing ___ dance. Yes, my life, it's bet - ter left to ___

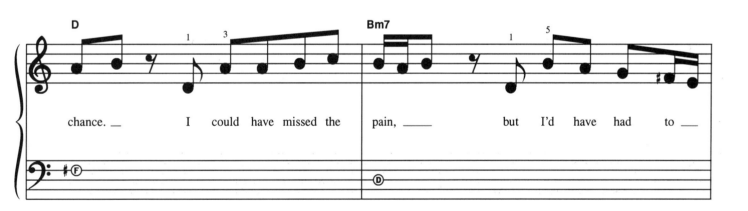

chance. ___ I could have missed the pain, ___ but I'd have had to ___

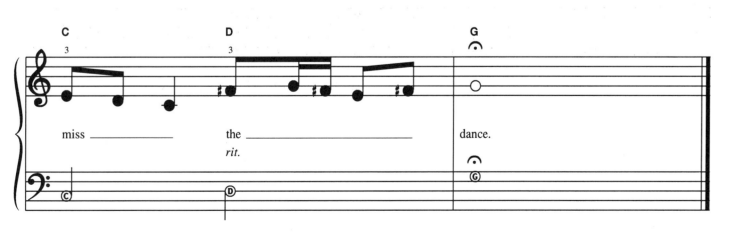

miss _____ the _____ dance.

rit.

DOWN AT THE TWIST AND SHOUT

Words and Music by
MARY CHAPIN CARPENTER

Fast COUNTRY TWO-BEAT

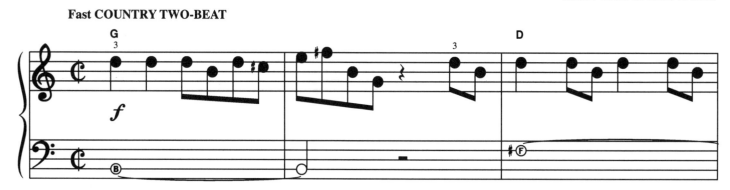

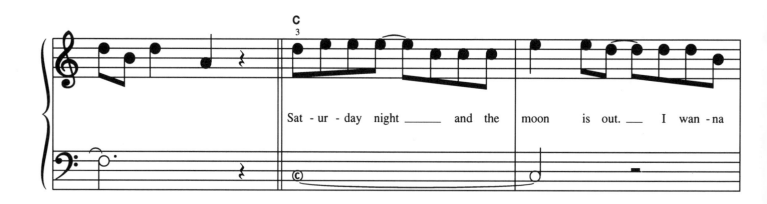

Sat - ur - day night _____ and the moon is out. ___ I wan - na

head on o - ver to the Twist and Shout, find a two - step part - ner and a

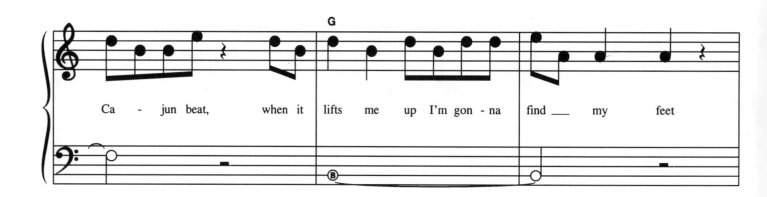

Ca - jun beat, when it lifts me up I'm gon - na find ___ my feet

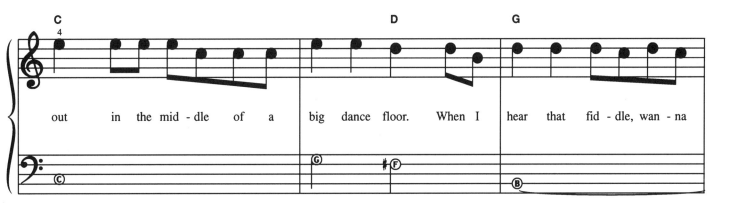

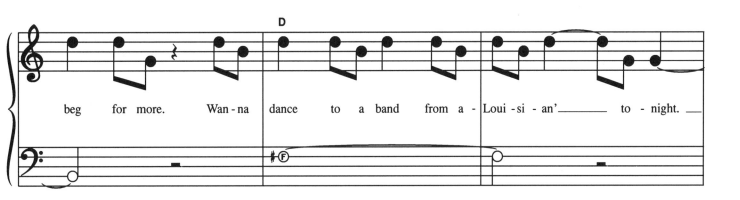

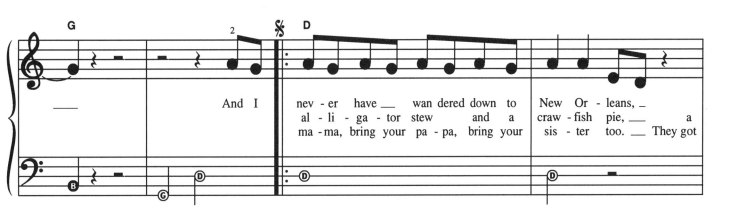

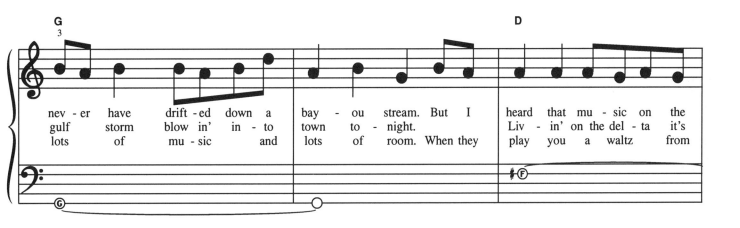

30

ra - di - o, and I swore some - day I was gon - na go: _____ down a -
quite a show. They got hur - ri - cane par - ties ev - 'ry time it blows. ___ But
a - nine - teen - ten, you're gon-na feel a lit - tle bit young a - gain. ___ Well, you

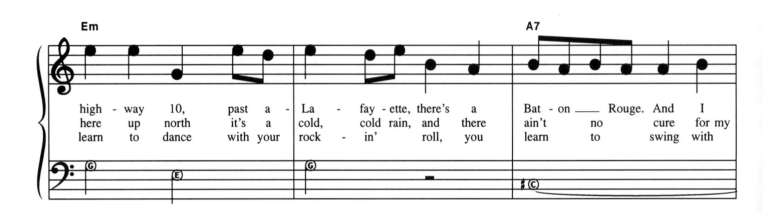

high - way 10, past a - La - fay - ette, there's a Bat - on _____ Rouge. And I
here up north it's a cold, cold rain, and there ain't no cure for my
learn to dance with your rock - in' roll, you learn to swing with

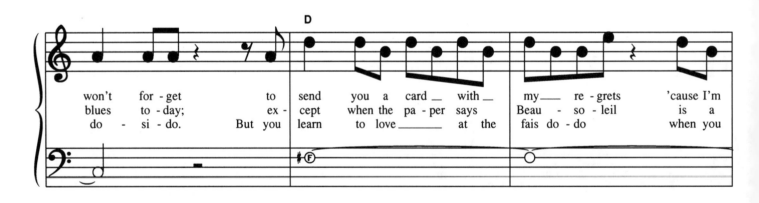

won't for - get to send you a card _ with _ my _ re - grets 'cause I'm
blues to - day; ex - cept when the pa - per says Beau - so - leil is a
do - si - do. But you learn to love _____ at the fais do - do when you

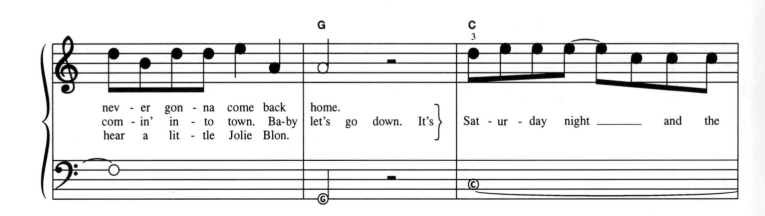

nev - er gon - na come back home.
com - in' in - to town. Ba-by let's go down. It's Sat - ur - day night _____ and the
hear a lit - tle Jolie Blon.

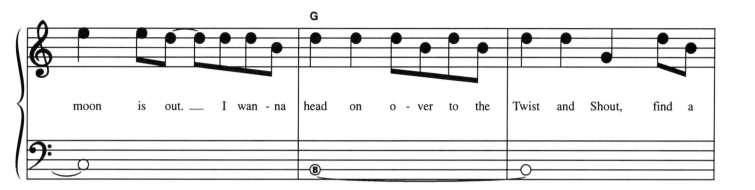

moon is out. ___ I wan - na head on o - ver to the Twist and Shout, find a

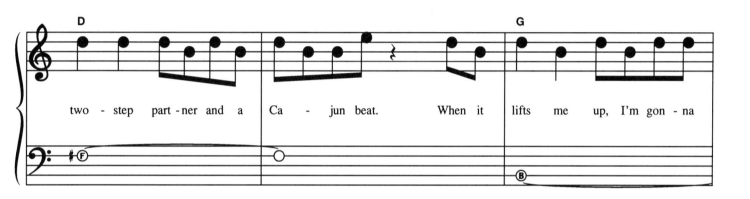

two - step part - ner and a Ca - jun beat. When it lifts me up, I'm gon - na

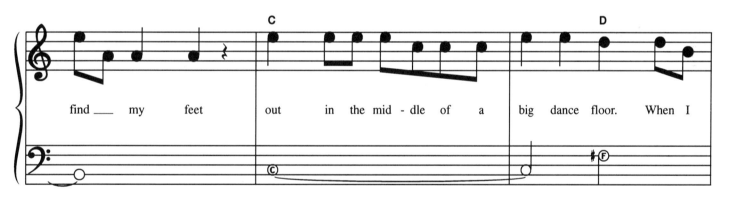

find ___ my feet out in the mid - dle of a big dance floor. When I

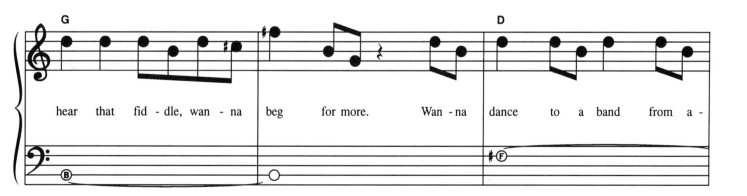

hear that fid - dle, wan - na beg for more. Wan - na dance to a band from a-

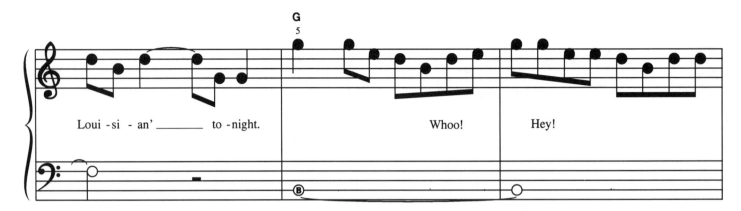

Loui - si - an' _____ to -night.   Whoo!   Hey!

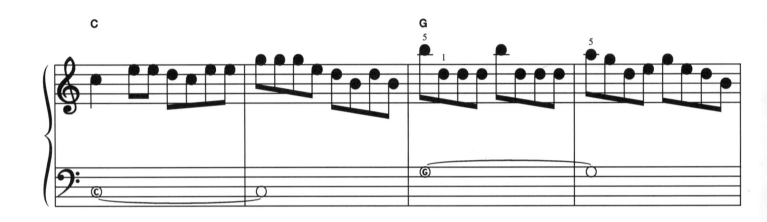

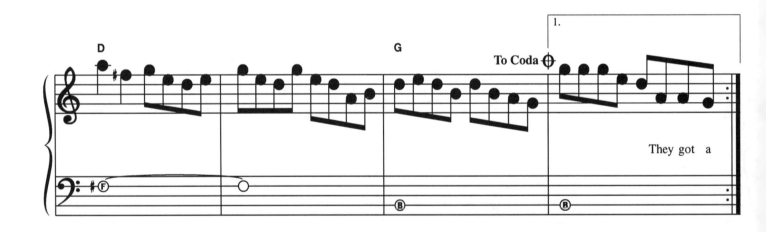

They got a

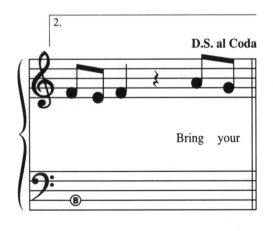

Bring your

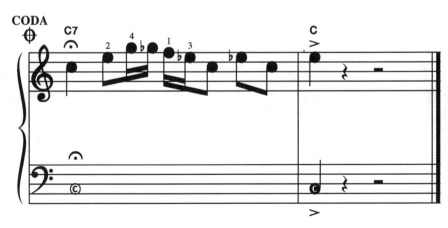

FOREVER AND EVER, AMEN

Words and Music by DON SCHLITZ
and PAUL OVERSTREET

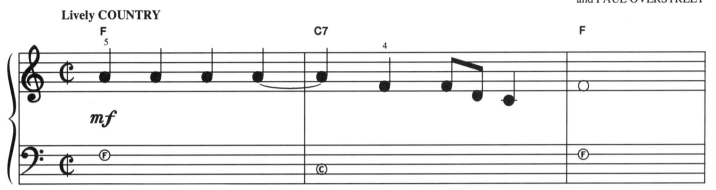

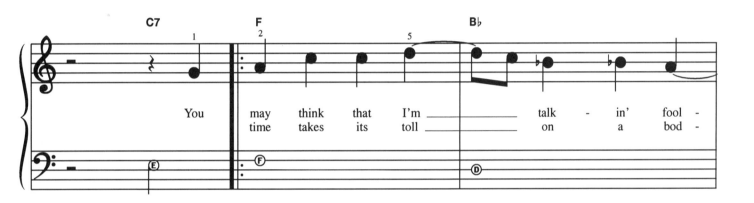

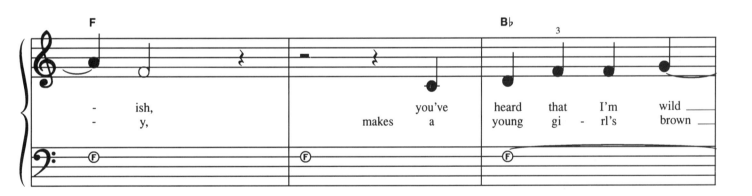

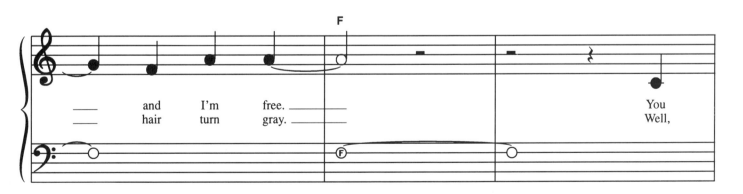

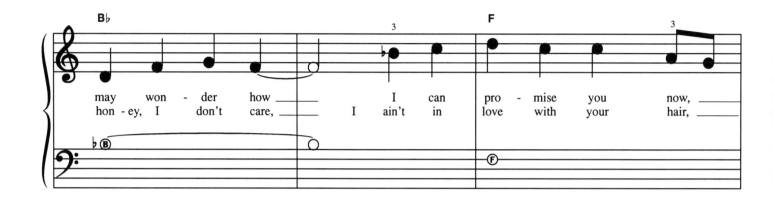

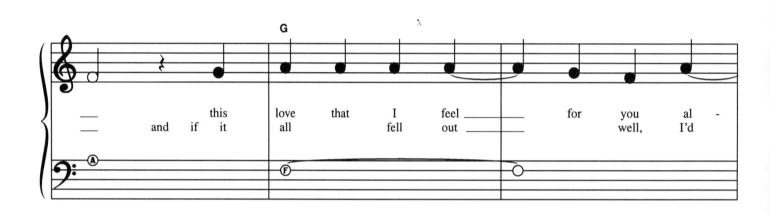

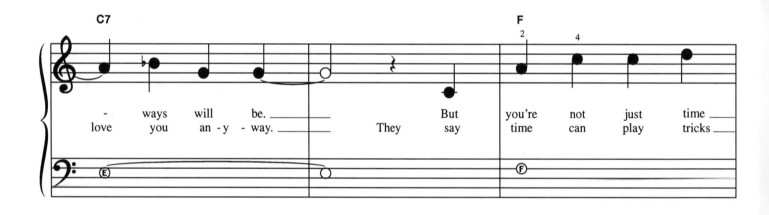

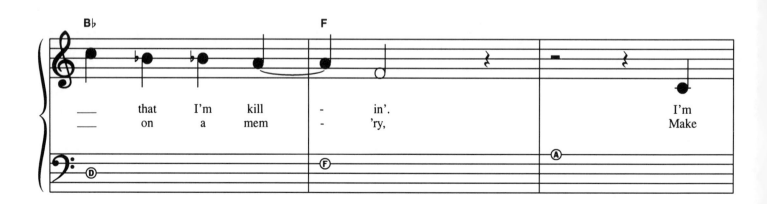

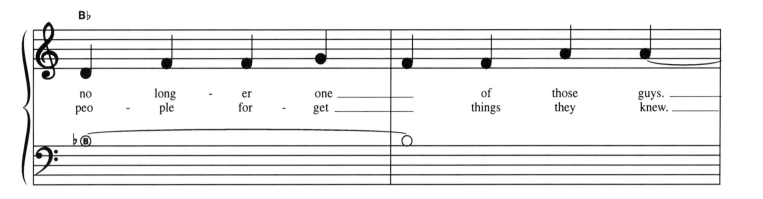

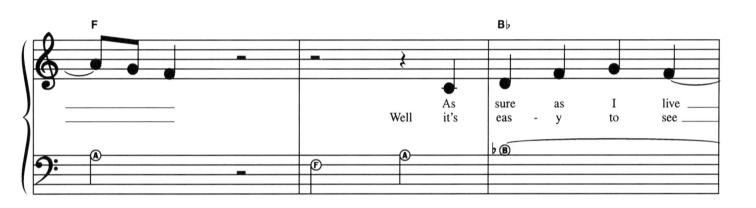

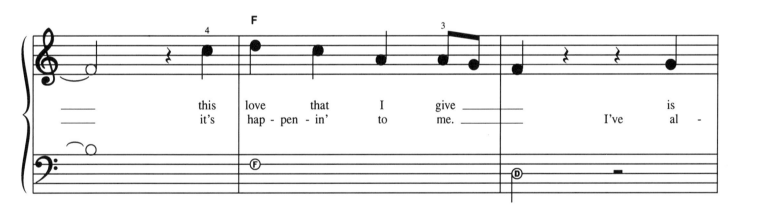

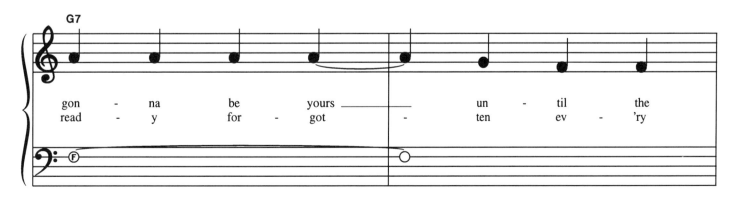

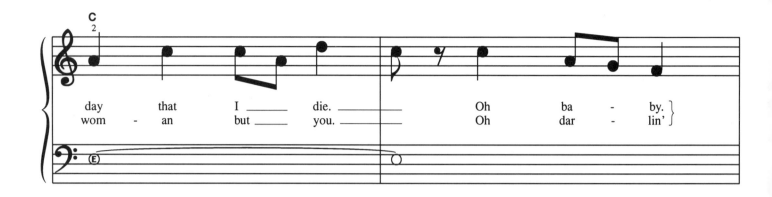

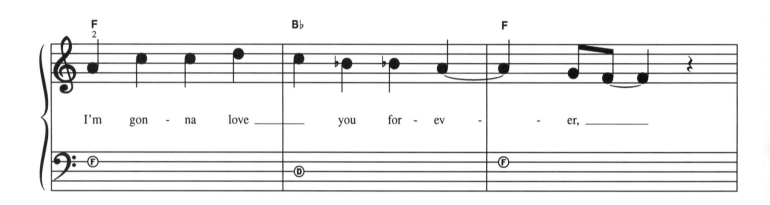

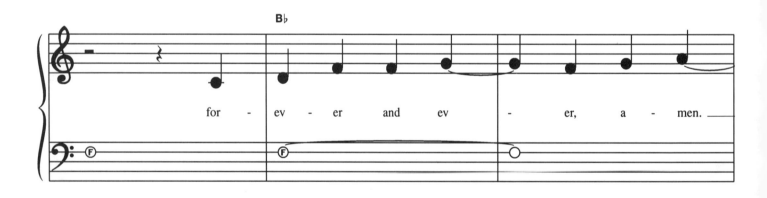

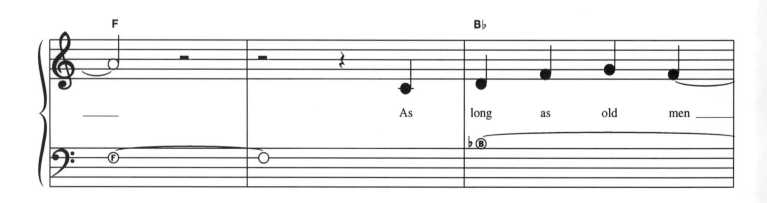

sit and talk a - bout ____ the weath - er, as

long as old wom - en sit and talk a - bout old ____

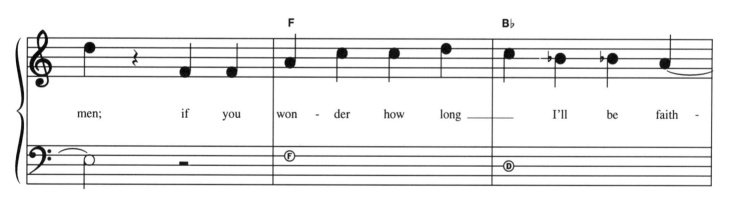

men; if you won - der how long ____ I'll be faith -

\- ful

I'll be hap - py to tell ____

Well just lis - ten to how ____

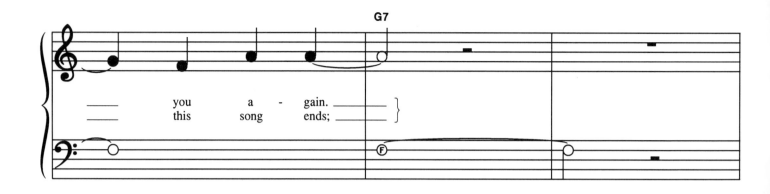

you a - gain.
this song ends;

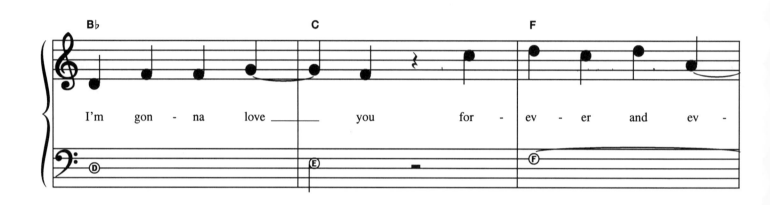

I'm gon - na love _____ you for - ev - er and ev -

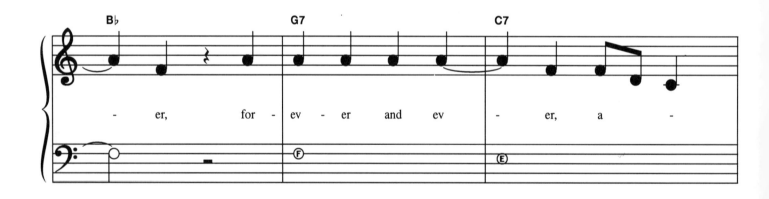

- er, for - ev - er and ev - er, a -

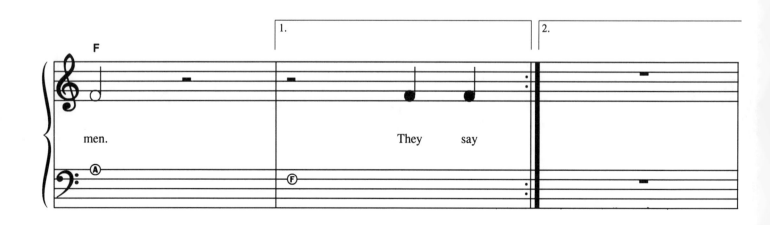

men.   They say

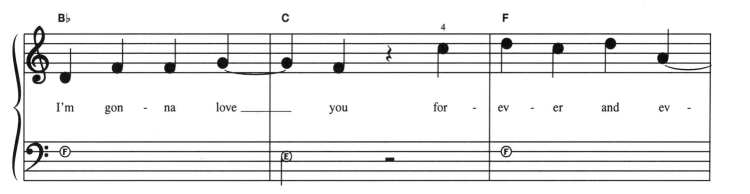

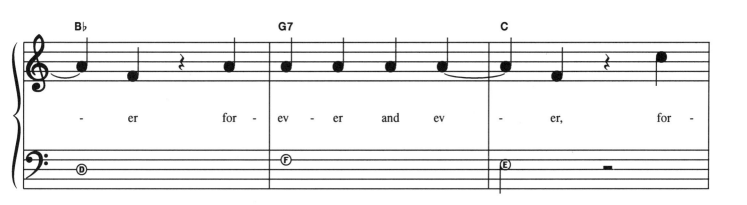

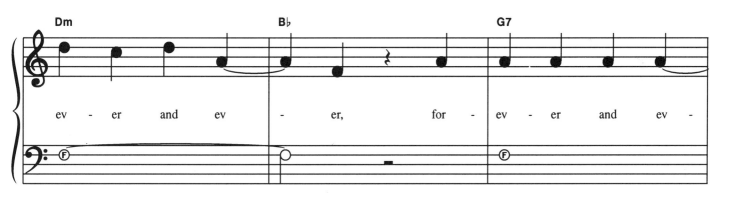

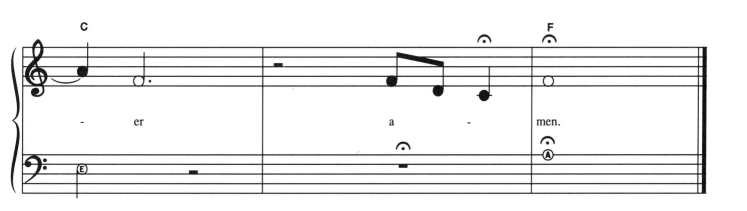

FRIENDS IN LOW PLACES

Words and Music by DeWAYNE BLACKWELL
and EARL BUD LEE

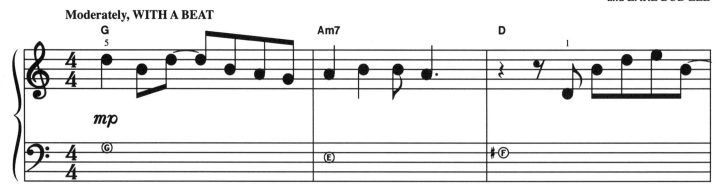

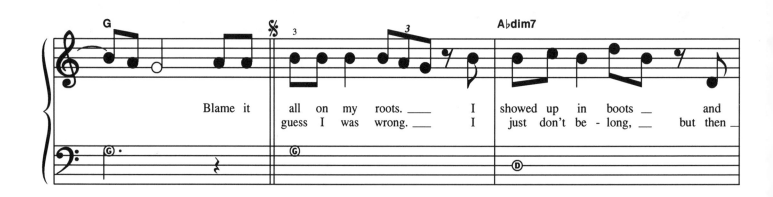

Blame it all on my roots. ___ I showed up in boots ___ and
guess I was wrong. ___ I just don't be-long, ___ but then

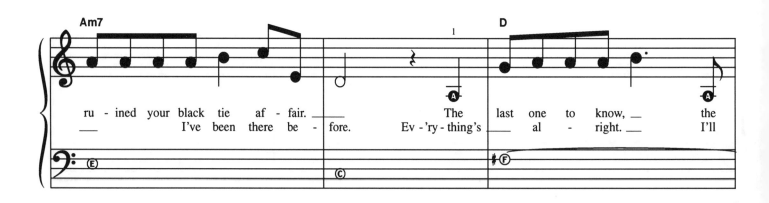

ru-ined your black tie af-fair. ___ The last one to know, ___ the
___ I've been there be-fore. Ev-'ry-thing's ___ al-right. ___ I'll

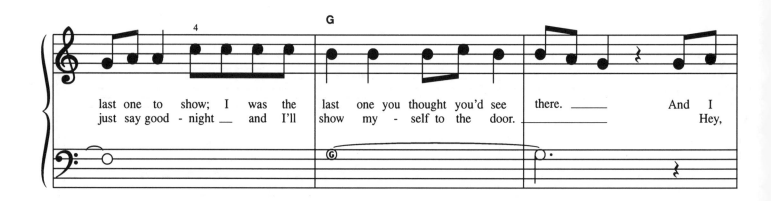

last one to show; I was the last one you thought you'd see there. ___ And I
just say good-night ___ and I'll show my-self to the door. ___ Hey,

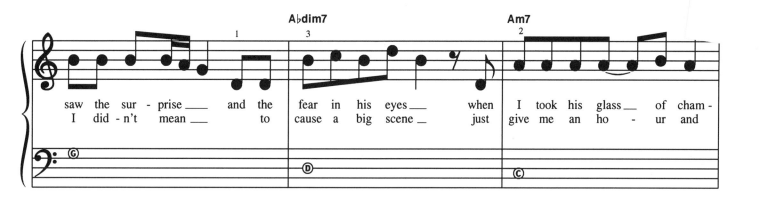

saw the sur - prise ___ and the fear in his eyes ___ when I took his glass ___ of cham -
I did - n't mean ___ to cause a big scene ___ just give me an ho - ur and

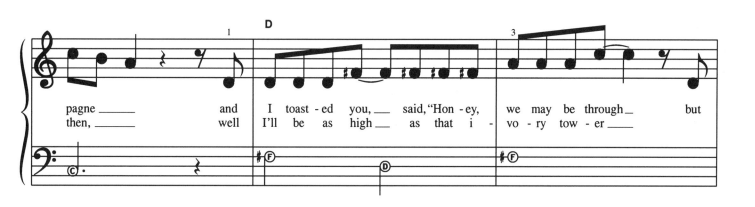

pagne ___ and I toast - ed you, ___ said, "Hon - ey, we may be through ___ but
then, ___ well I'll be as high ___ as that i - vo - ry tow - er ___

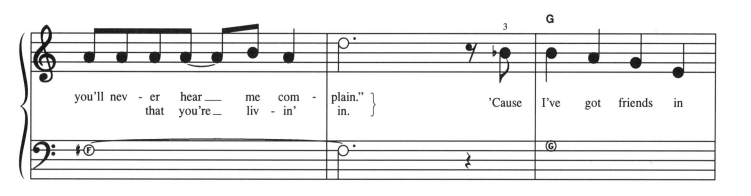

you'll nev - er hear ___ me com - plain." } 'Cause I've got friends in
that you're ___ liv - in' in.

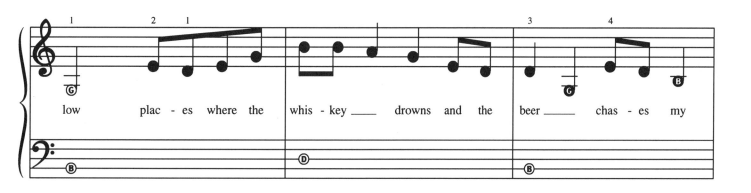

low plac - es where the whis - key ___ drowns and the beer ___ chas - es my

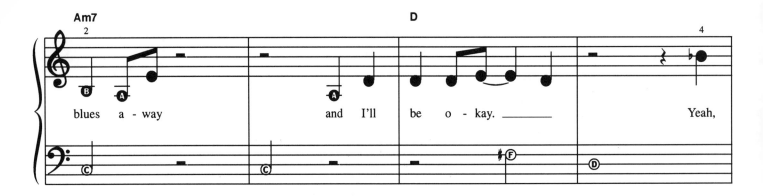

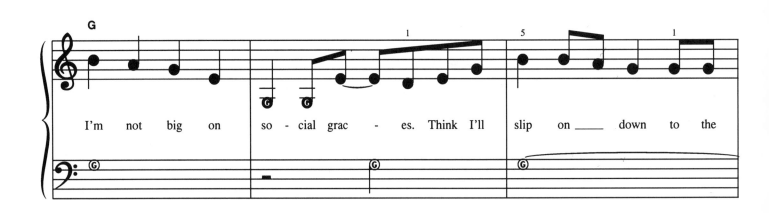

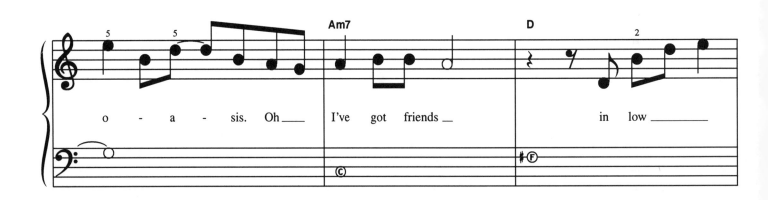

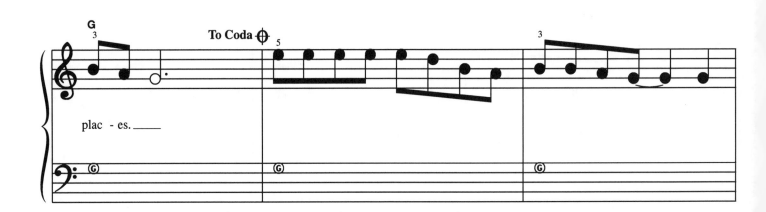

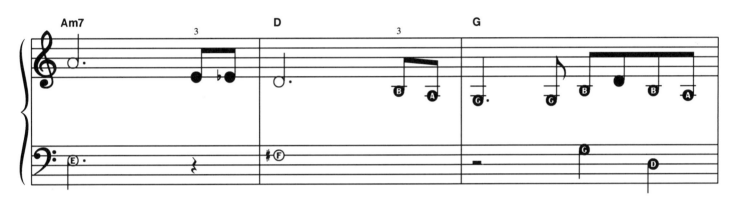

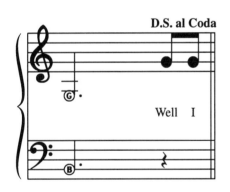

Well I

I've got friends in

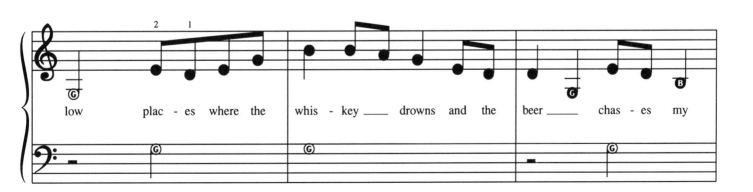

low plac - es where the whis - key ____ drowns and the beer ____ chas - es my

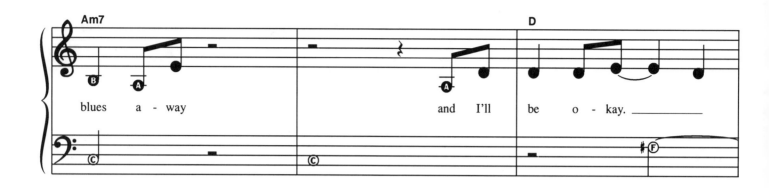

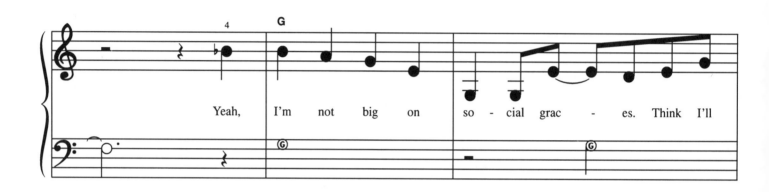

GOD BLESS THE U.S.A.

Words and Music by
LEE GREENWOOD

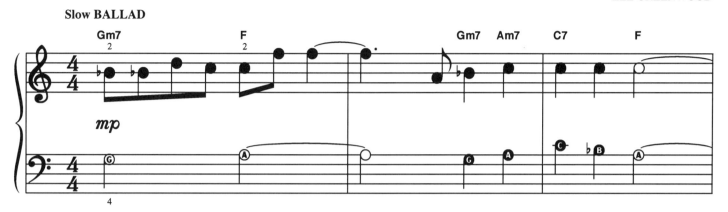

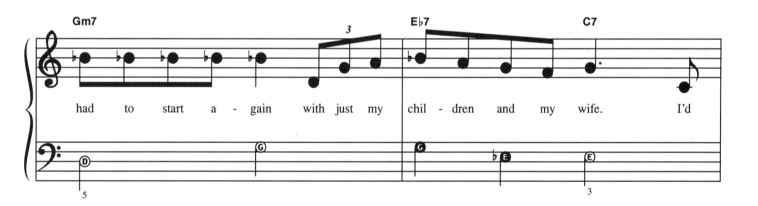

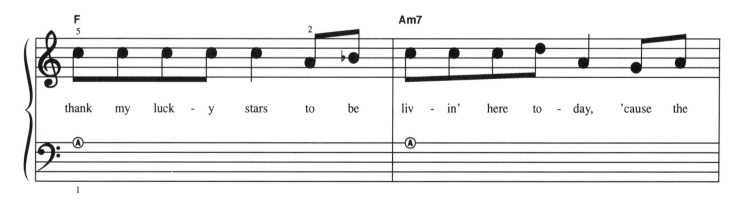

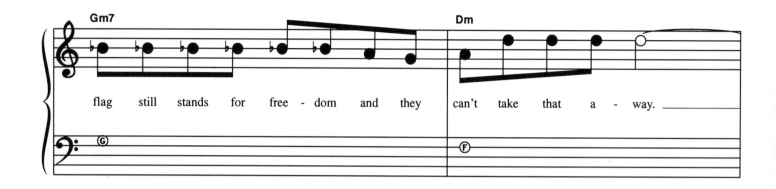

flag still stands for free - dom and they can't take that a - way. ___

Chorus

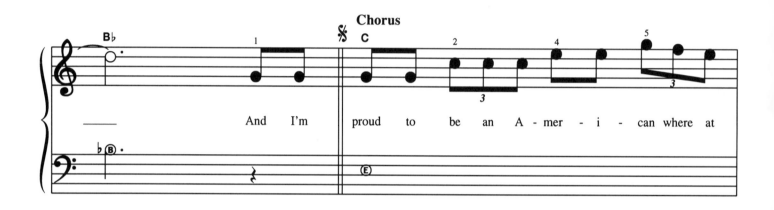

___ And I'm proud to be an A - mer - i - can where at

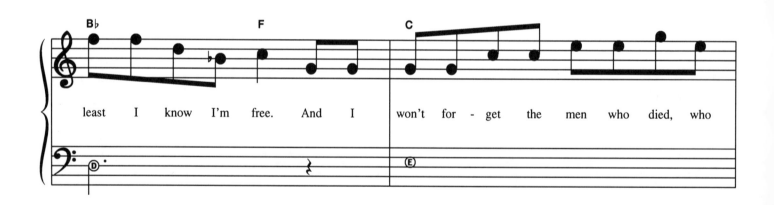

least I know I'm free. And I won't for - get the men who died, who

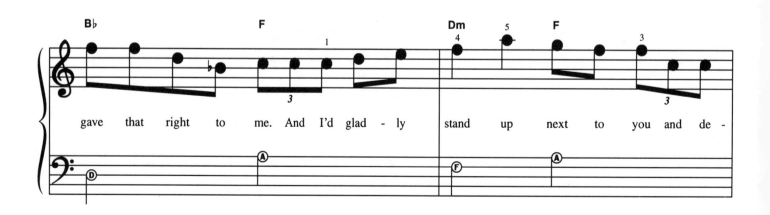

gave that right to me. And I'd glad - ly stand up next to you and de -

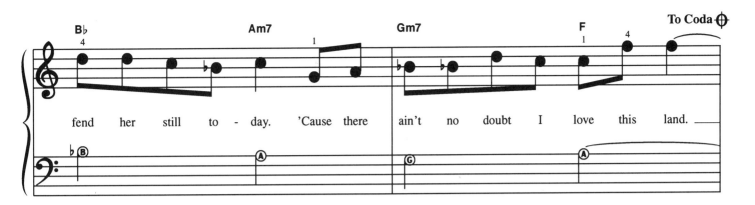

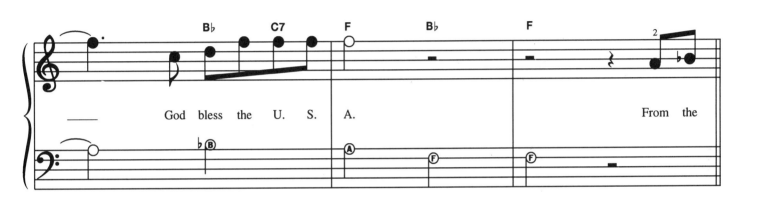

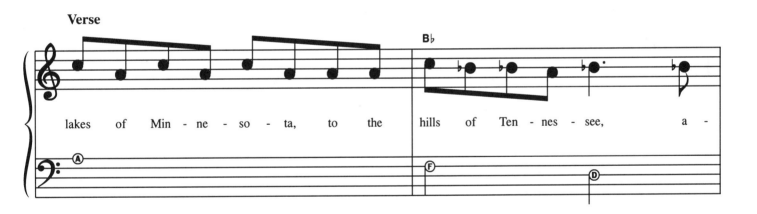

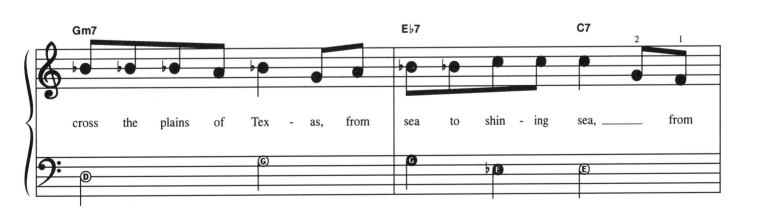

De - troit down to Hous - ton and New York to L. A. Well, there's

pride in ev - 'ry A - mer - i - can heart and it's time to stand and say ____

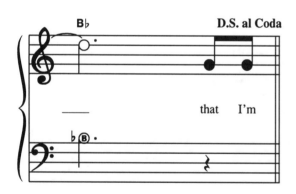

____ that I'm

____ God bless the U. S.

A. ____ And I'm proud to be an A - mer - i - can where at

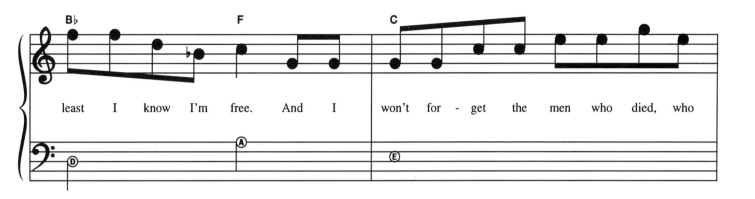

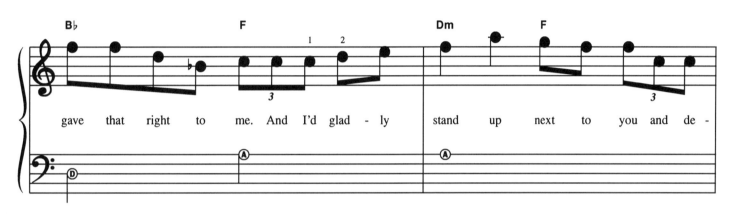

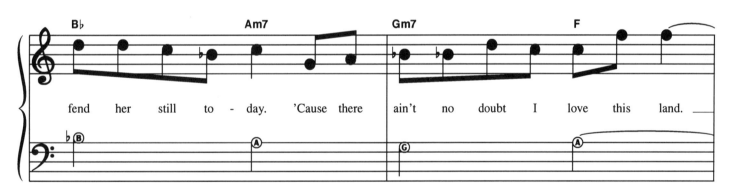

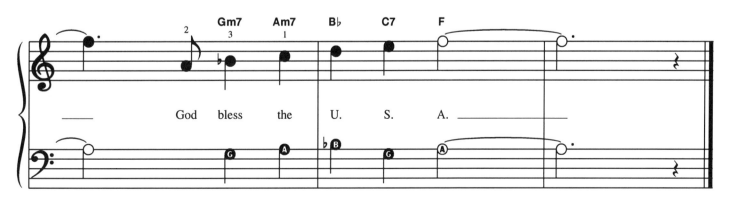

GRANDPA
(Tell Me 'Bout The Good Old Days)

Words and Music by
JAMIE O'HARA

Medium SLOW COUNTRY

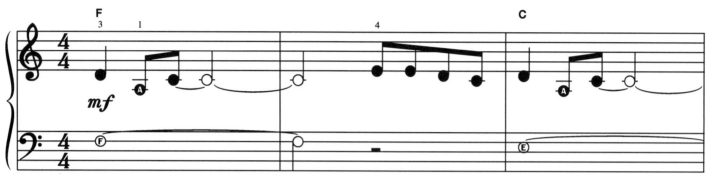

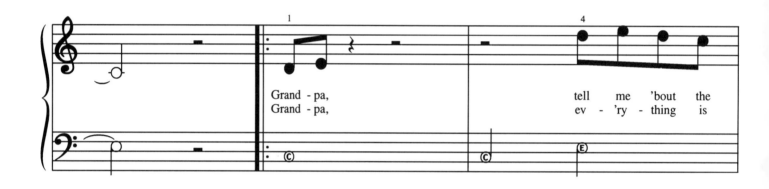

Grand - pa,
Grand - pa,

tell me 'bout the
ev - 'ry - thing is

good old days.
chang - in' fast.

Some - times _____ it
We call _____ it

feels like
prog - ress,

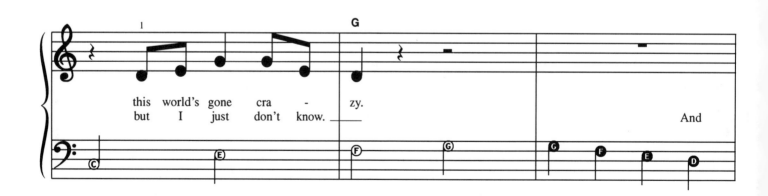

this world's gone cra - zy.
but I just don't know. _____

And

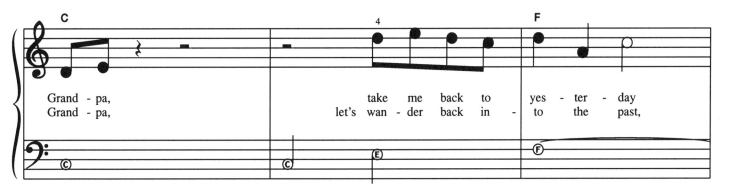

Grand - pa, take me back to yes - ter - day
Grand - pa, let's wan - der back in - to the past,

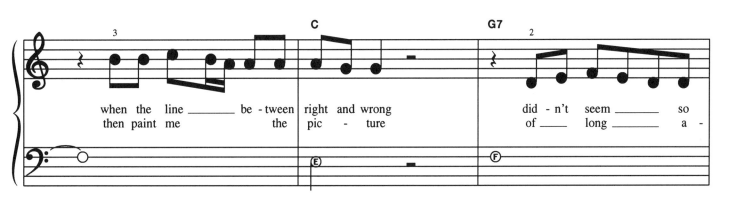

when the line ____ be - tween right and wrong
then paint me the pic - ture

did - n't seem ____ so
of ____ long ____ a -

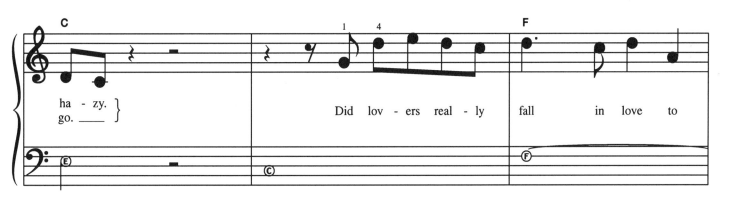

ha - zy.
go. ____

Did lov - ers real - ly fall in love to

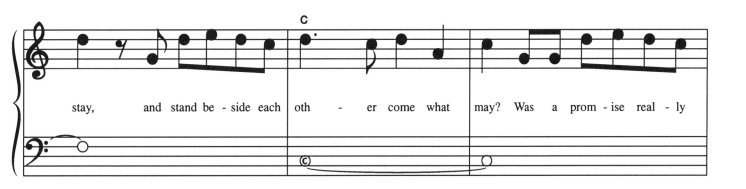

stay, and stand be - side each oth - er come what may? Was a prom - ise real - ly

some - thing peo - ple ___ kept, not just some - thing they would say? ___ (and then forget)

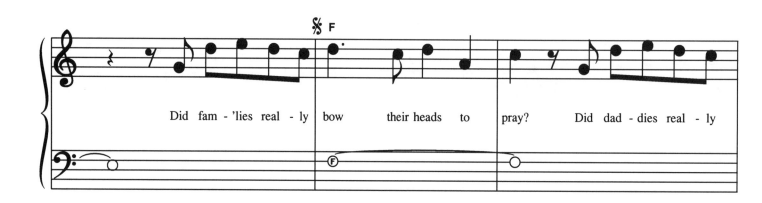

Did fam - 'lies real - ly bow their heads to pray? Did dad - dies real - ly

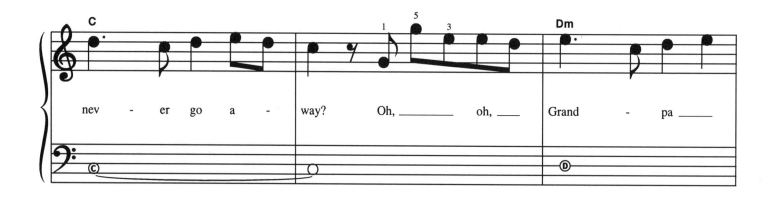

nev - er go a - way? Oh, ___ oh, ___ Grand - pa ___

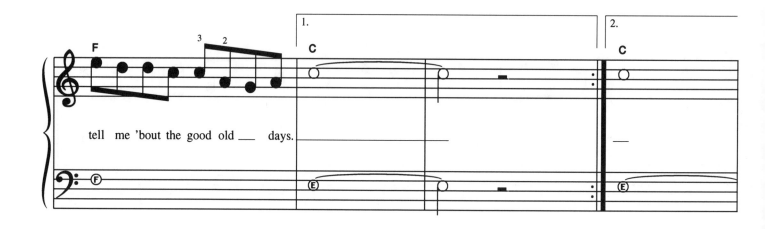

tell me 'bout the good old ___ days.

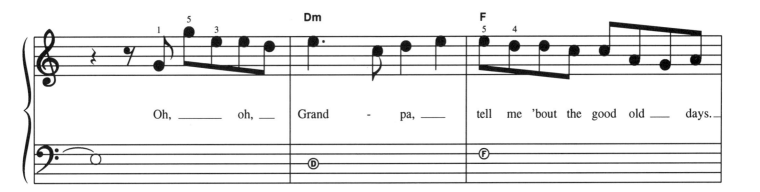

Oh, _____ oh, _____ Grand - pa, _____ tell me 'bout the good old _____ days.

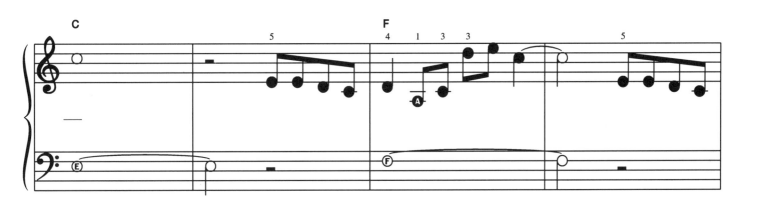

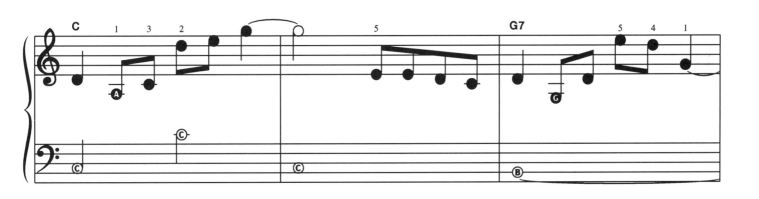

D.S. and Fade

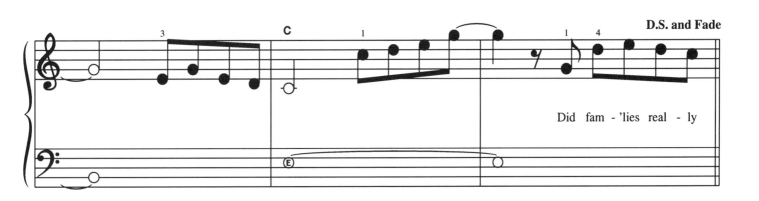

Did fam - 'lies real - ly

I FEEL LUCKY

Words and Music by MARY CHAPIN CARPENTER
and DON SCHLITZ

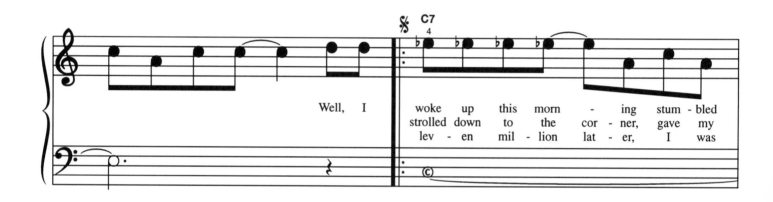

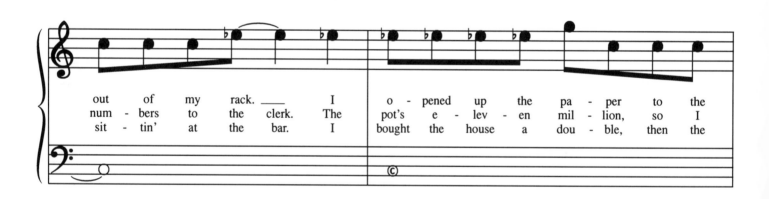

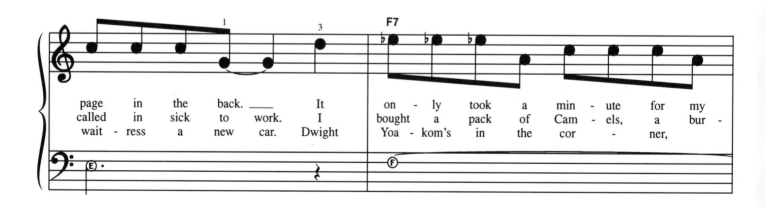

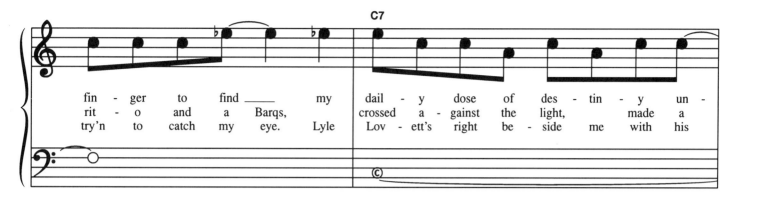

fin - ger to find _____ my
rit - o and a Barqs,
try'n to catch my eye. Lyle

dail - y dose of des - tin - y un -
crossed a - gainst the light, made a
Lov - ett's right be - side me with his

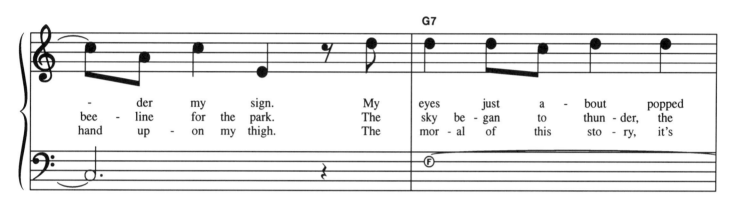

- der my sign. My
bee - line for the park. The
hand up - on my thigh. The

eyes just a - bout popped
sky be - gan to thun - der, the
mor - al of this sto - ry, it's

out - a my head. _____ It said, "The
wind be - gan to moan. I heard a
sim - ple but it's true. Hey, the

stars are stacked a - gainst you, girl.
voice a - bove me say - in', "Girl, you'd
stars might lie, but the

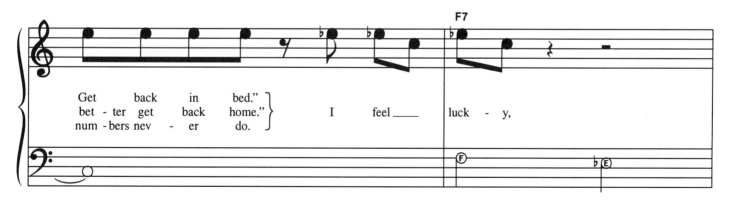

Get back in bed."
bet - ter get back home."   I feel _____ luck - y,
num - bers nev - er do.

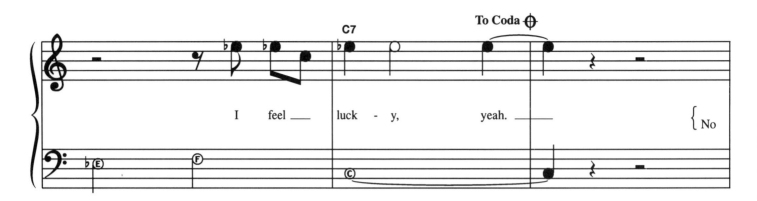

I feel ___ luck - y, yeah. ___ { No

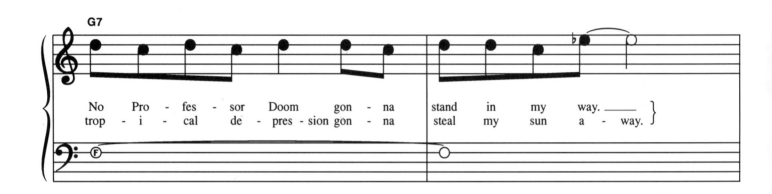

No Pro - fes - sor Doom gon - na stand in my way. ___
trop - i - cal de - pres - sion gon - na steal my sun a - way. }

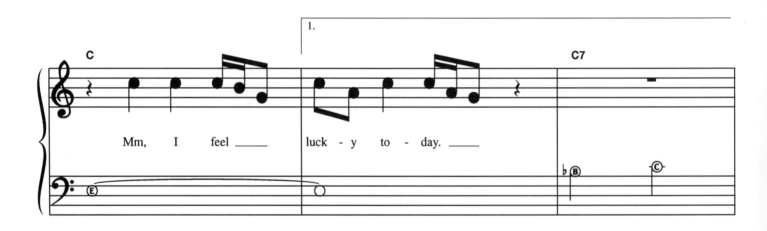

Mm, I feel ___ luck - y to - day. ___

Well, I luck - y to - day. ___

Now e -

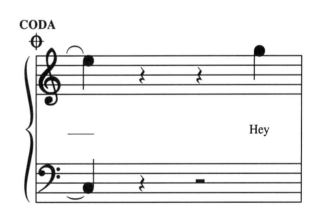

Hey

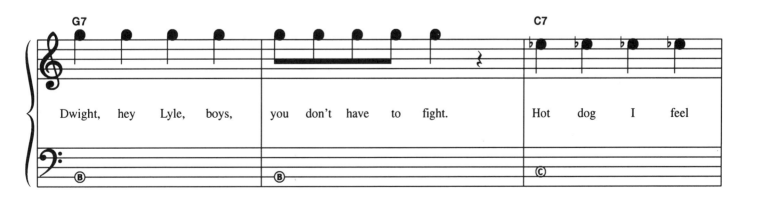

Dwight, hey Lyle, boys, you don't have to fight. Hot dog I feel

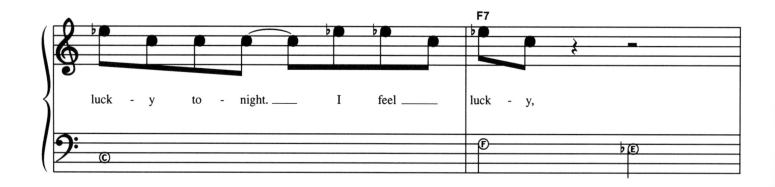

luck - y to - night. ____ I feel ____ luck - y,

I feel ____ luck - y, yeah. ____

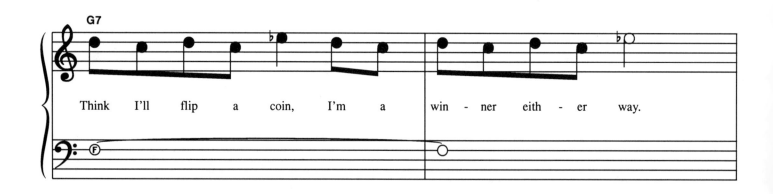

Think I'll flip a coin, I'm a win - ner eith - er way.

Mm, I feel ____ luck - y to - day. ____

KING OF THE ROAD

Words and Music by
ROGER MILLER

Moderate BOUNCE TEMPO

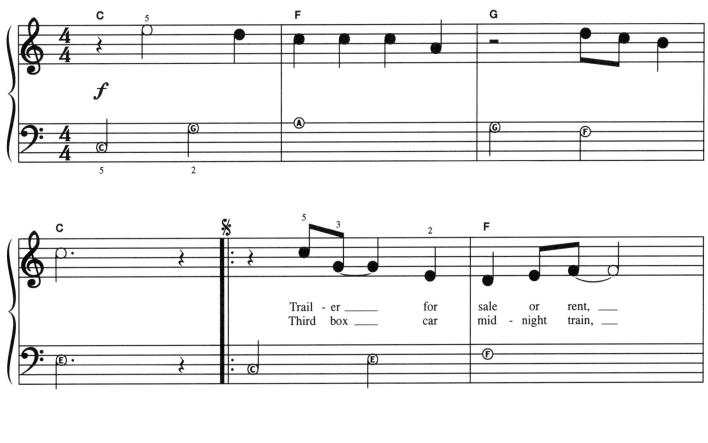

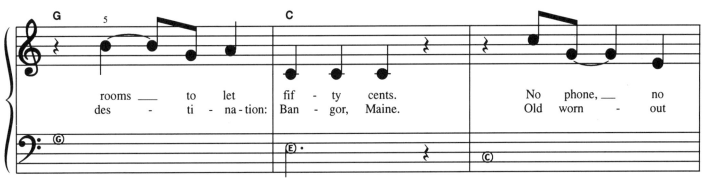

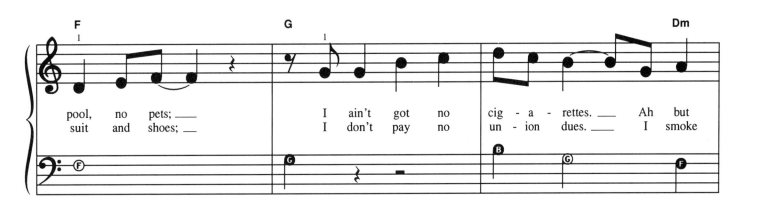

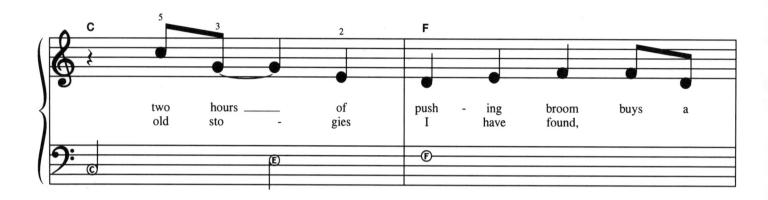

two hours _____ of push - ing broom buys a
old sto - gies I have broom found,

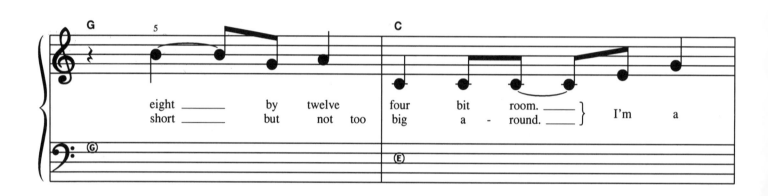

eight _____ by twelve four bit room. _____ } I'm a
short _____ but not too big a - round. _____

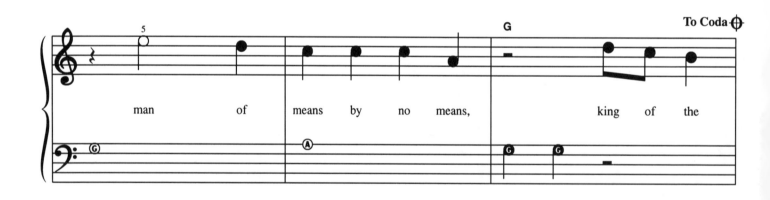

man of means by no means, king of the

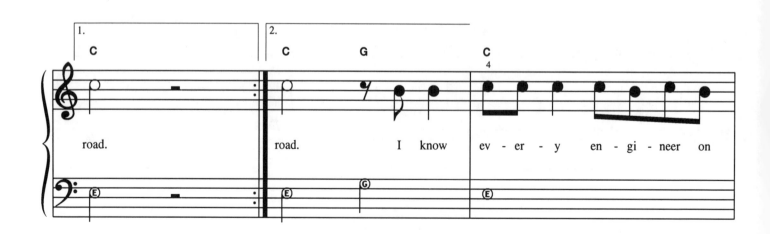

road.　　road.　　I know ev - er - y en - gi - neer on

ev - er - y train, all of the chil - dren and

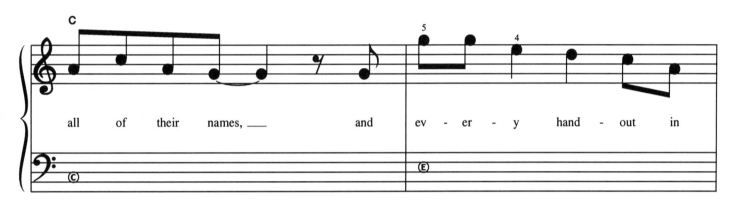

all of their names, ___ and ev - er - y hand - out in

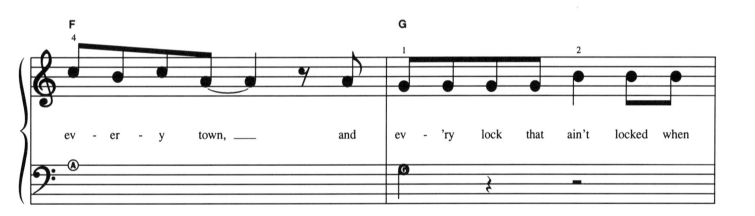

ev - er - y town, ___ and ev - 'ry lock that ain't locked when

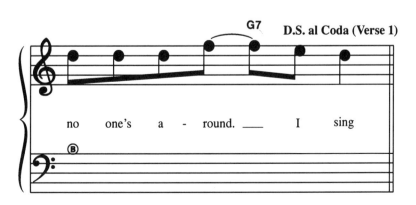

no one's a - round. ___ I sing

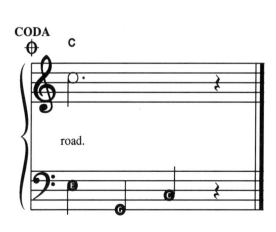

road.

LOVE CAN BUILD A BRIDGE

Words and Music by JOHN JARVIS,
PAUL OVERSTREET and NAOMI JUDD

Moderately SLOW

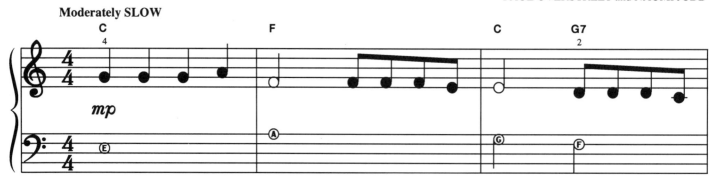

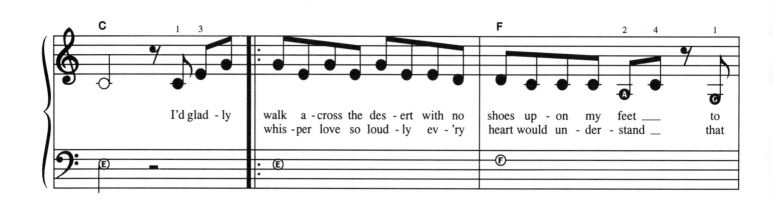

I'd glad - ly
walk a - cross the des - ert with no
whis - per love so loud - ly ev - 'ry
shoes up - on my feet ___ to
heart would un - der - stand ___ that

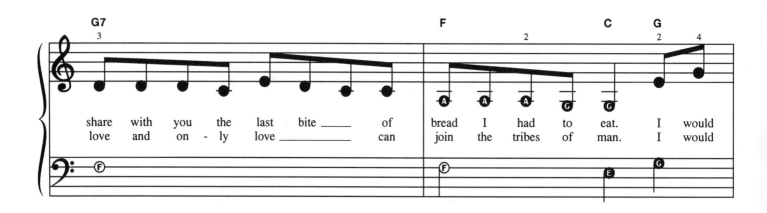

share with you the last bite ___ of
love and on - ly love ___ can
bread I had to eat. I would
join the tribes of man. I would

swim out to save you in your
give my heart's de - sire ___ so
sea of bro - ken dreams, ___ when
that you might see. ___ The

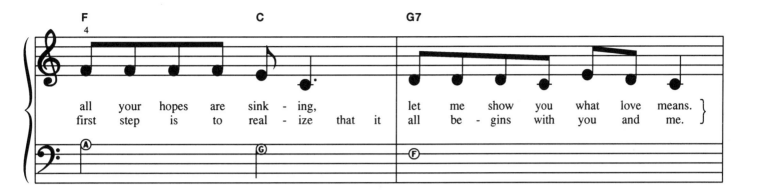

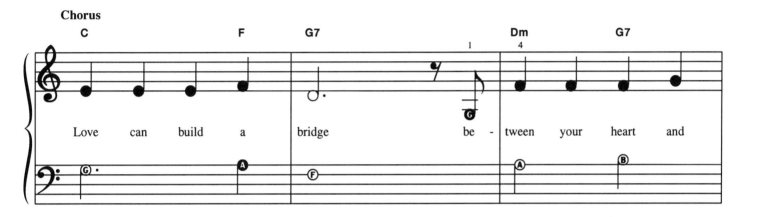

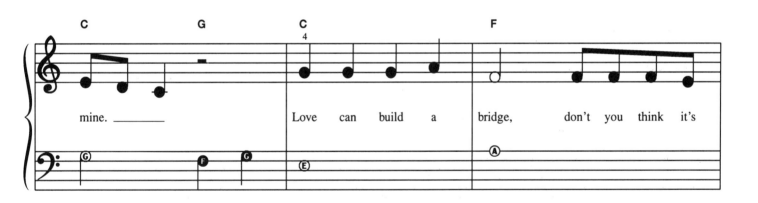

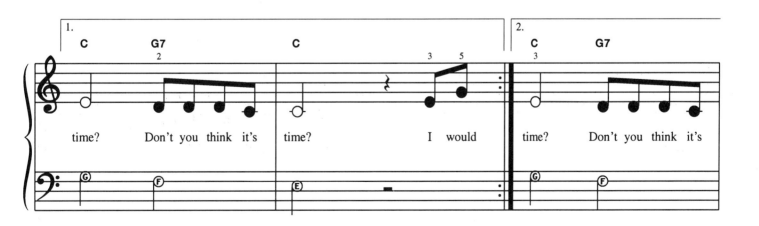

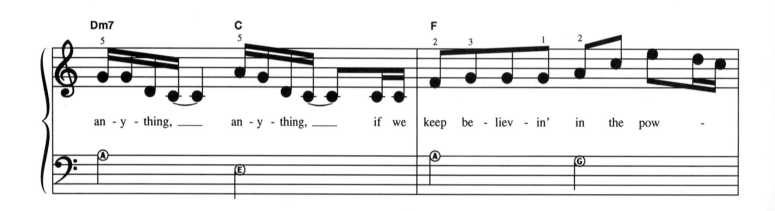

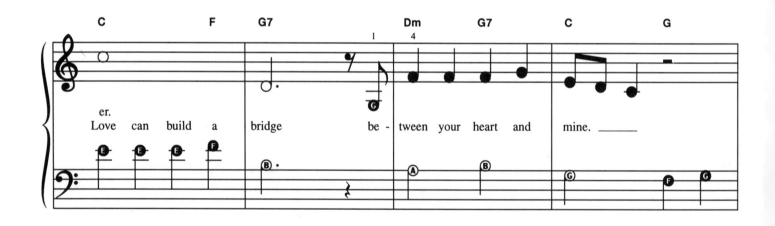

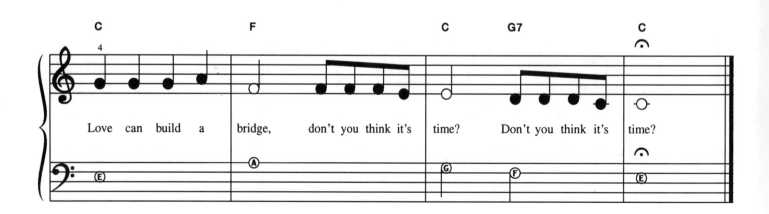

MAMMAS DON'T LET YOUR BABIES GROW UP TO BE COWBOYS

Words and Music by ED BRUCE
and PATSY BRUCE

Country WALTZ

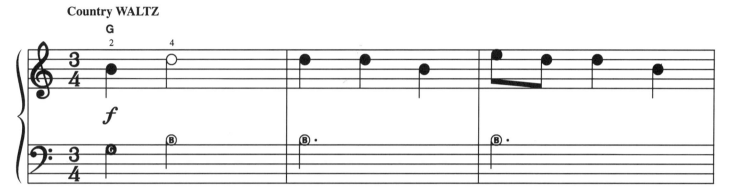

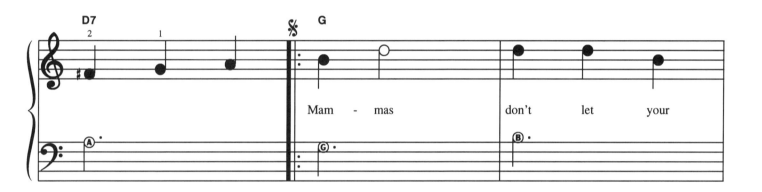

Mam - mas don't let your

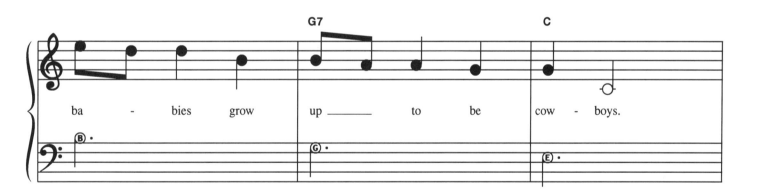

ba - bies grow up _____ to be cow - boys.

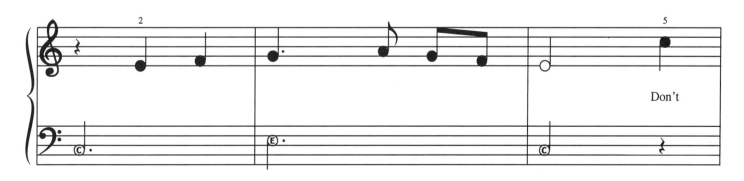

Don't

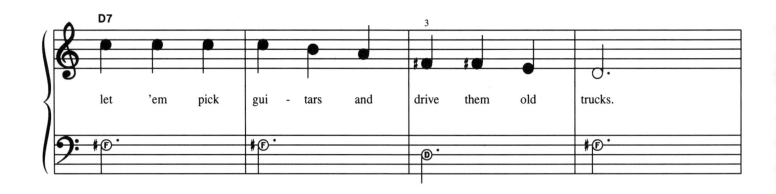

let 'em pick gui - tars and drive them old trucks.

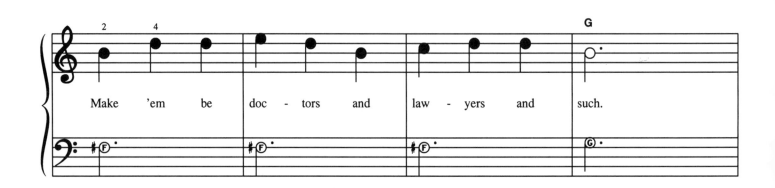

Make 'em be doc - tors and law - yers and such.

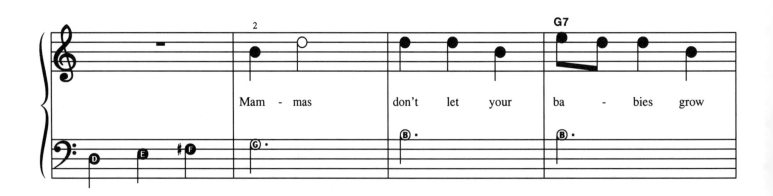

Mam - mas don't let your ba - bies grow

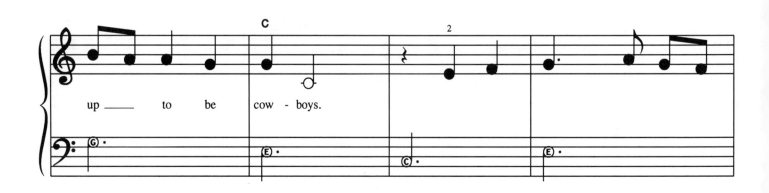

up ___ to be cow - boys.

'Cause they'll nev - er stay ___ home, and they're al - ways a -

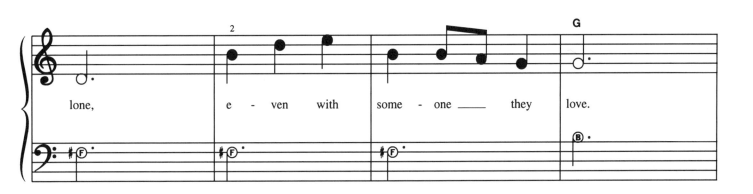

lone, e - ven with some - one ___ they love.

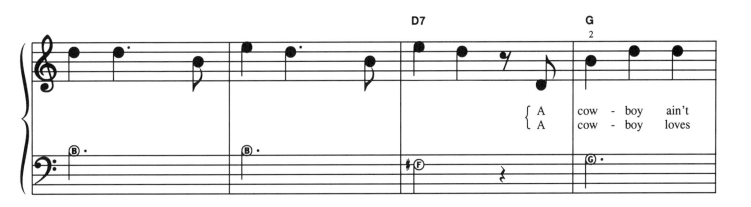

A cow - boy ain't
A cow - boy loves

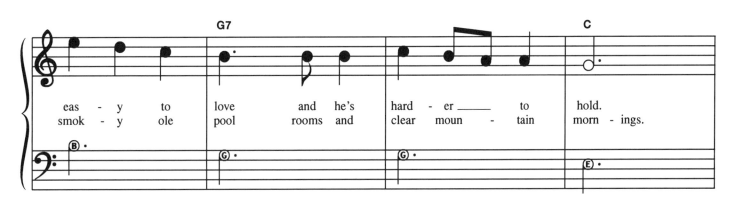

eas - y to love and he's hard - er ___ to hold.
smok - y ole pool rooms and clear moun - tain morn - ings.

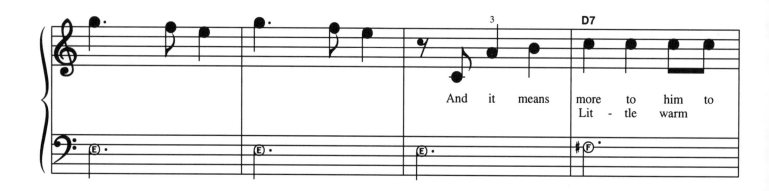

And it means more to him to
Lit - tle warm

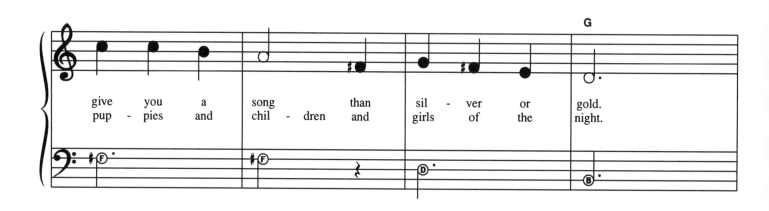

give you a song than sil - ver or gold.
pup - pies and chil - dren and girls of or the night.

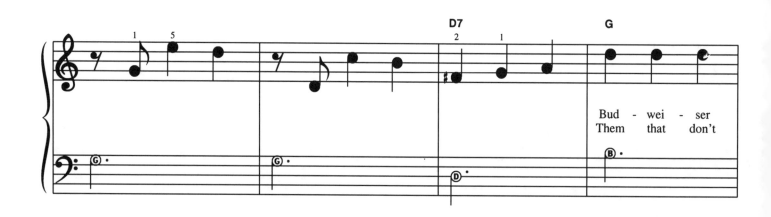

Bud - wei - ser
Them that don't

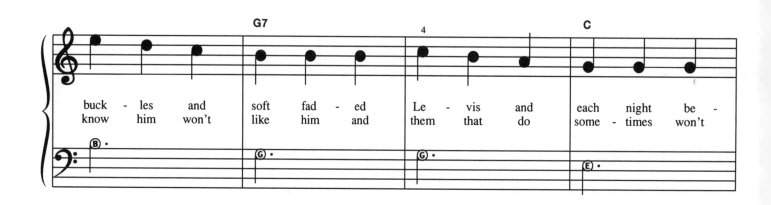

buck - les and soft fad - ed Le - vis and each night be -
know him and won't like him and them that and do some - times won't

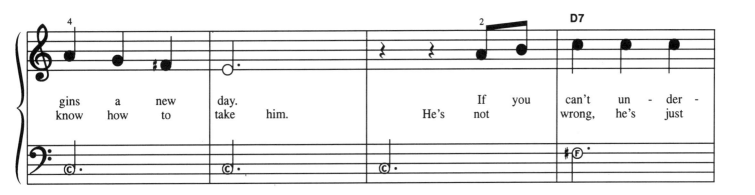

gins a new day. | He's not | If you can't un - der -
know how to take him. | wrong, he's just

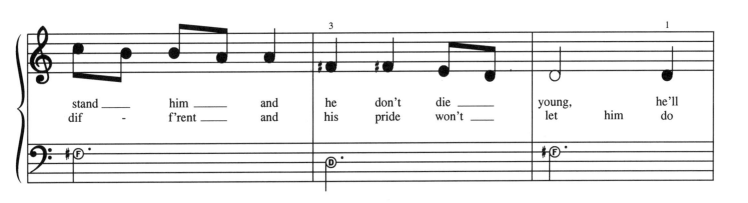

stand ____ him ____ and | he don't die ____ | young, he'll
dif - f'rent ____ and | his pride won't ____ | let him do

prob - a - bly | just ride ____ a - way.
things to make | you think ____ he's right.

NO ONE ELSE ON EARTH

Words and Music by SAM LORBER,
STEWART HARRIS and JILL COLUCCI

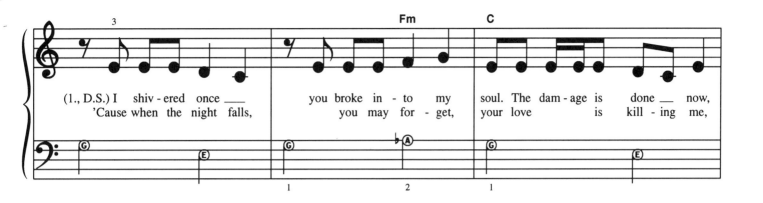

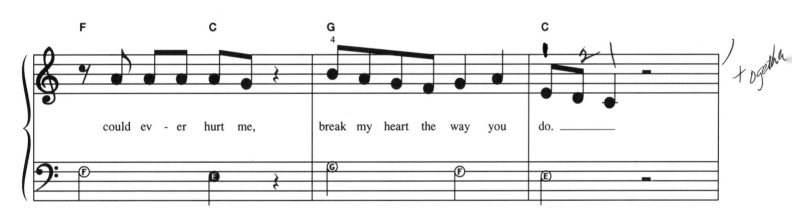

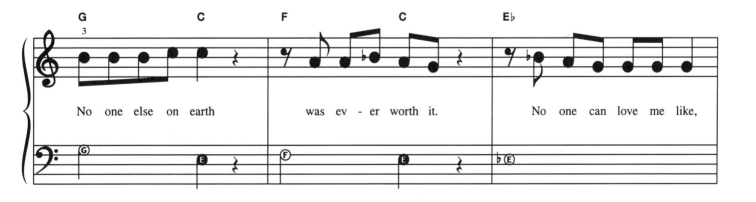

no one can love me like you.

you.

D.S. al Coda

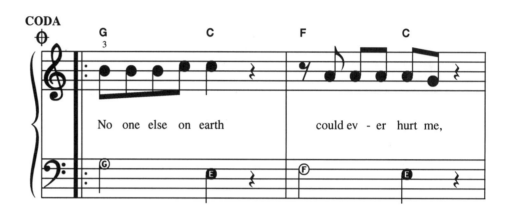

CODA

No one else on earth could ev - er hurt me,

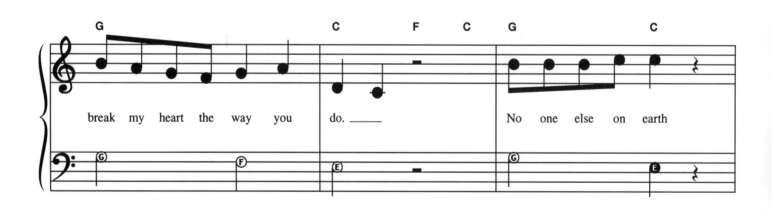

break my heart the way you do. ____ No one else on earth

Repeat and Fade

was ev - er worth it. No one can love me like, no one can hurt me like,

ROCKY TOP

Words and Music by BOUDLEAUX BRYANT
and FELICE BRYANT

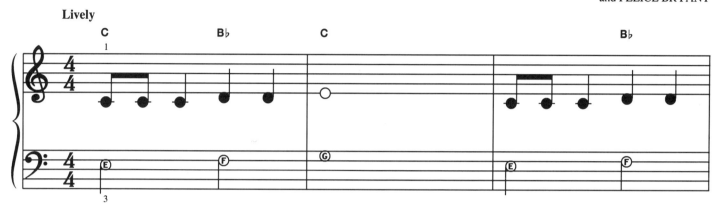

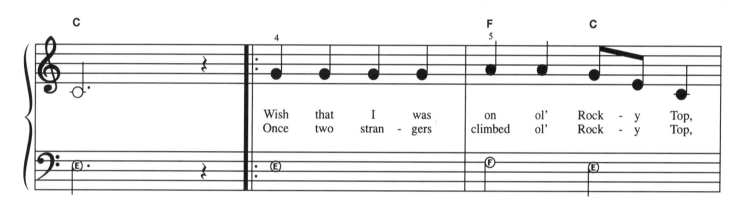

Wish that I was on ol' Rock - y Top,
Once two stran - gers climbed ol' Rock - y Top,

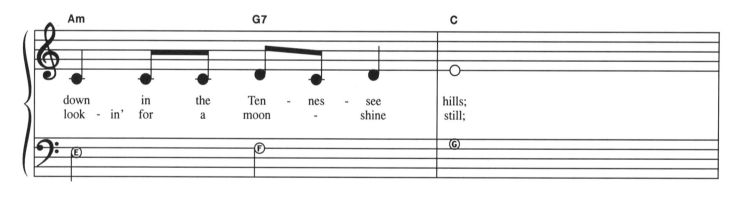

down in the Ten - nes - see hills;
look - in' for a moon - shine still;

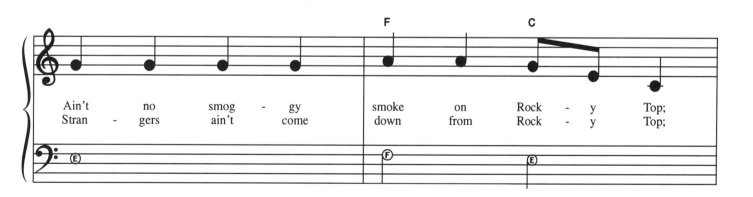

Ain't no smog - gy smoke on Rock - y Top;
Stran - gers ain't come down from Rock - y Top;

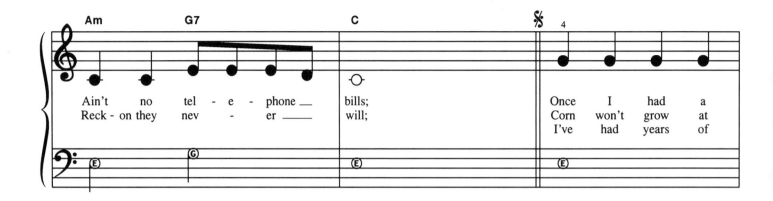

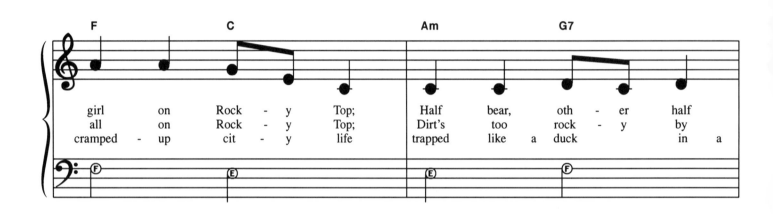

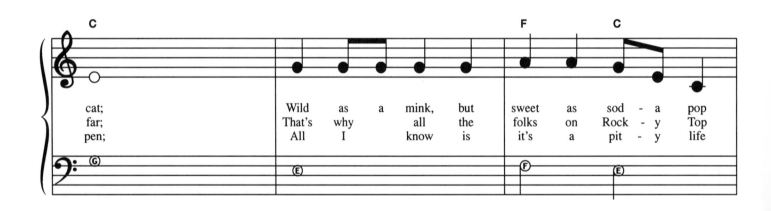

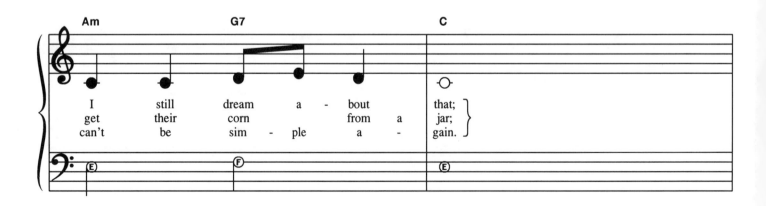

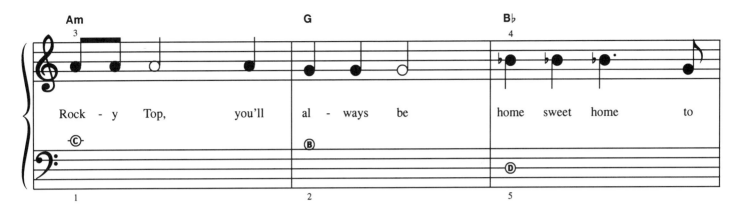

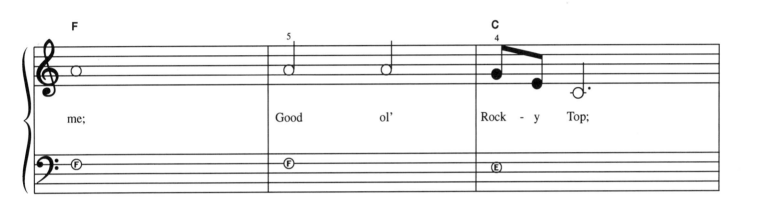

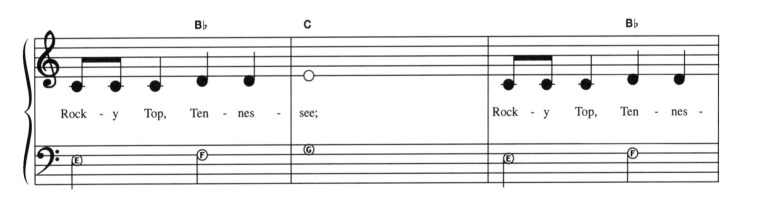

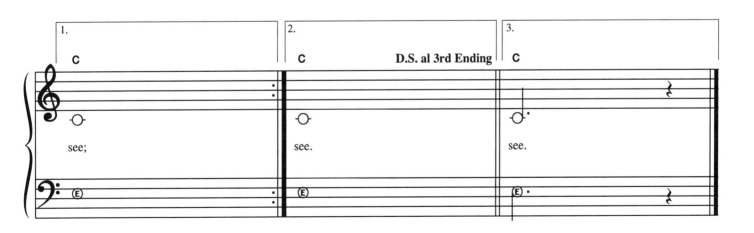

STAND BY YOUR MAN

Words and Music by TAMMY WYNETTE
and BILLY SHERRILL

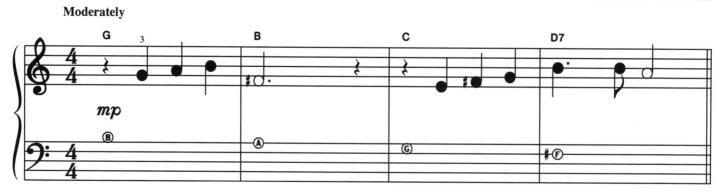

Some - times it's hard _____ to be a wom - an, _____
But if you love him you'll for - give him, _____

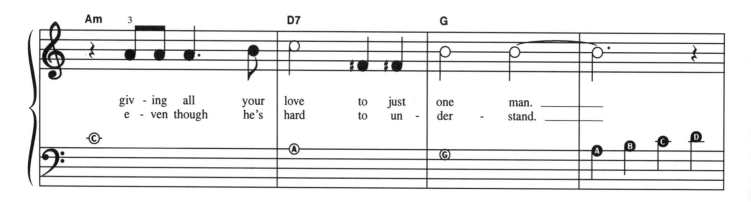

giv - ing all your love to just one man. _____
e - ven though he's hard to un - der - stand. _____

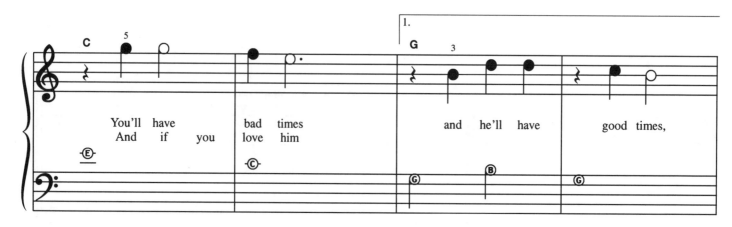

You'll have bad times and he'll have good times,
And if you love him

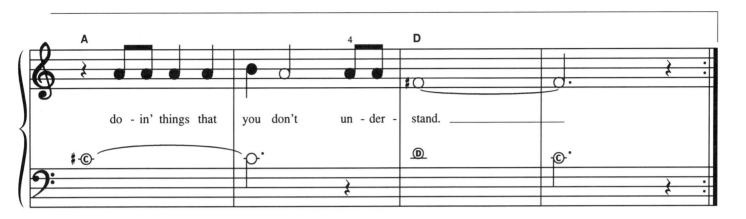

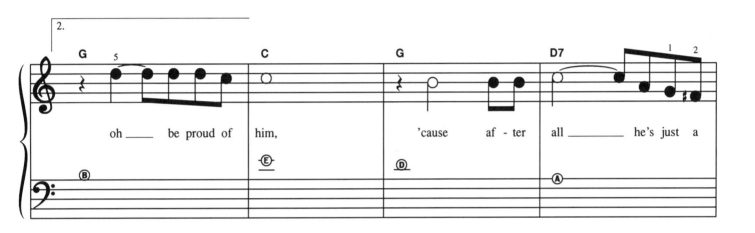

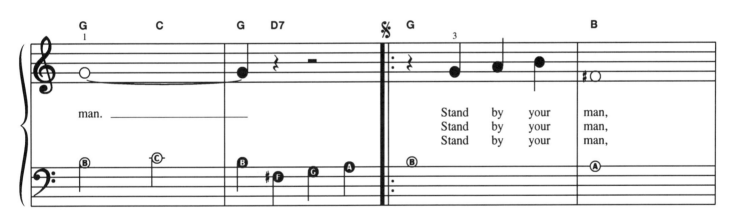

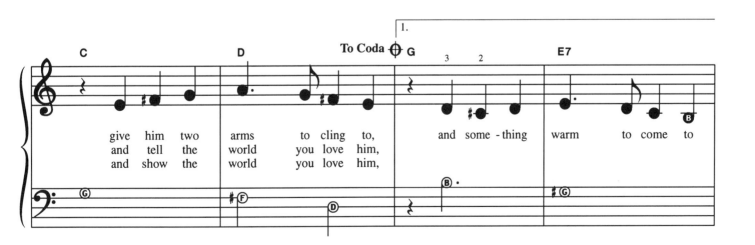

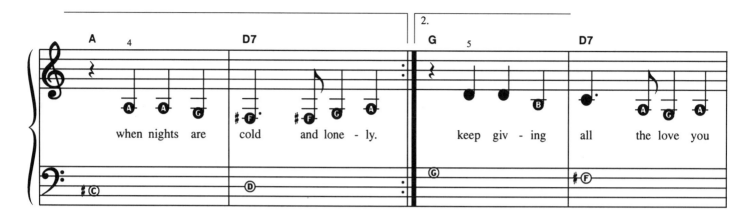

when nights are cold and lone - ly.
keep giv - ing all the love you

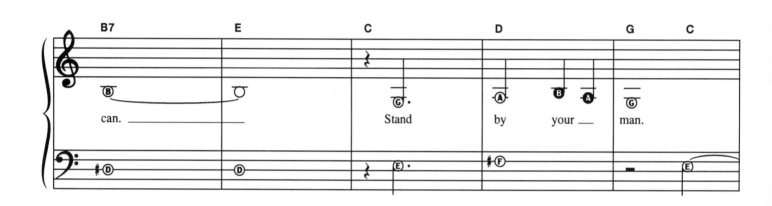

can. _____ Stand by your _____ man.

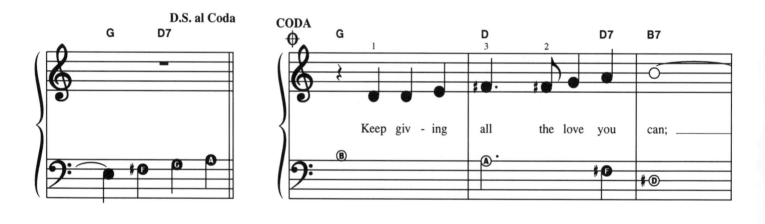

D.S. al Coda

CODA

Keep giv - ing all the love you can; _____

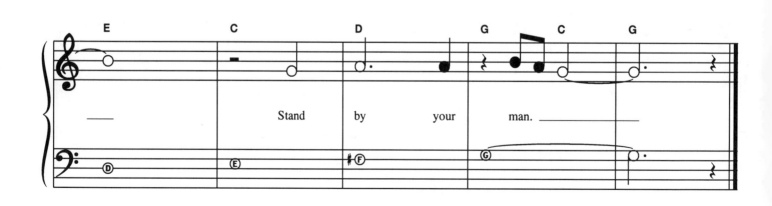

_____ Stand by your man. _____

WE SHALL BE FREE

By STEPHANIE DAVIS
and GARTH BROOKS

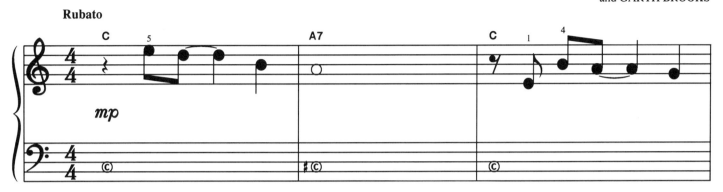

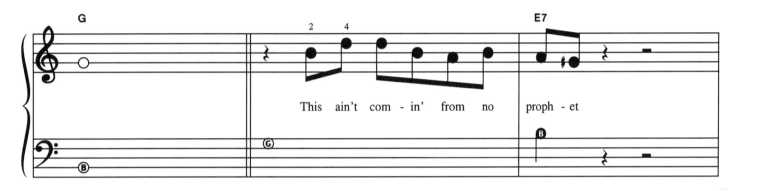

This ain't com - in' from no proph - et

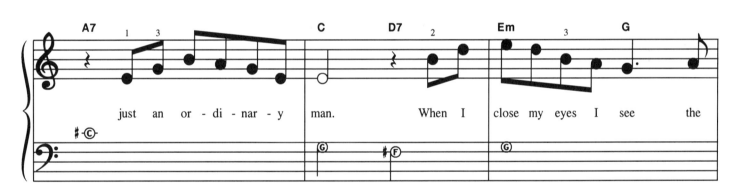

just an or - di - nar - y man. When I close my eyes I see the

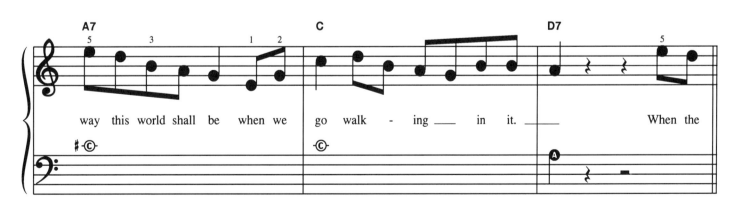

way this world shall be when we go walk - ing ___ in it. ___ When the

Moderate GOSPEL FEEL

last child cries ___ for a crust of bread, ___ when the last man dies _____ for just

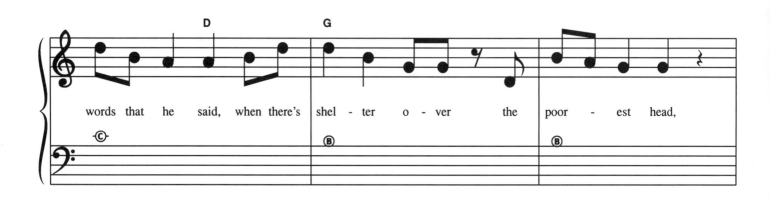

words that he said, when there's shel - ter o - ver the poor - est head,

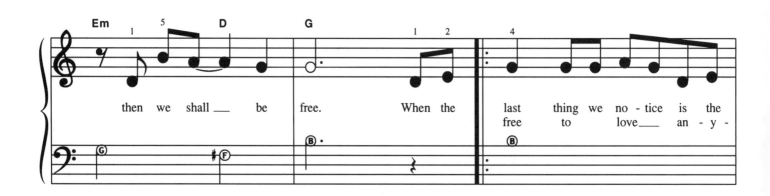

then we shall ___ be free. When the last thing we no - tice is the
free to love___ an - y -

col - or of skin, _____ and the first thing we look for is the
one we choose, ___ when this world's big e - nough for

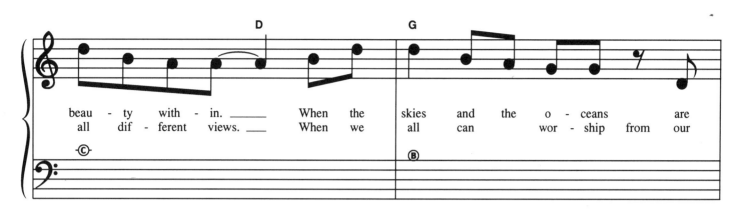

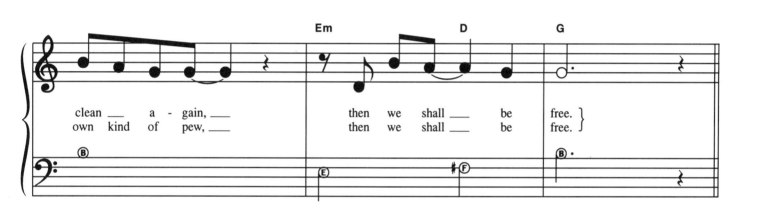

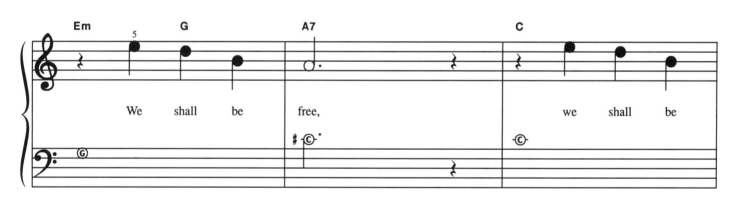

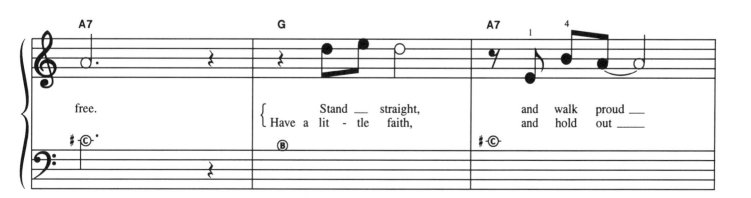

1.
'cause we shall ___ be free. ___ ___ When we're

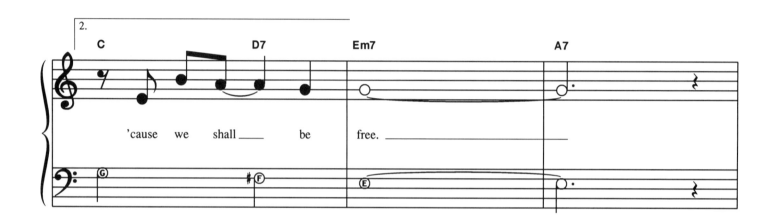

2.
'cause we shall ___ be free. ___ ___

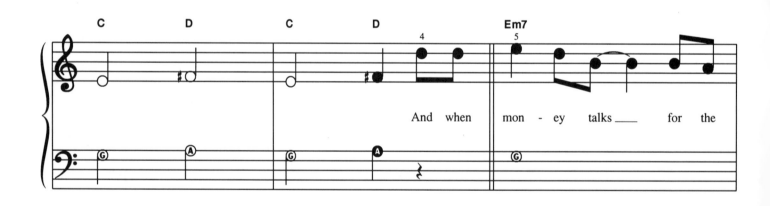

And when mon - ey talks ___ for the

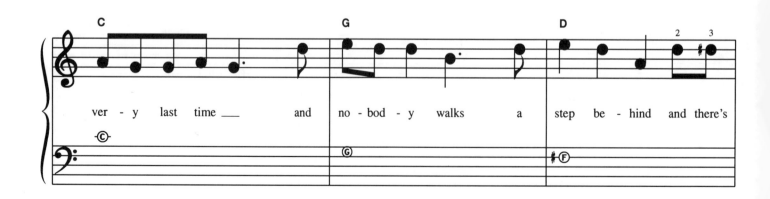

ver - y last time ___ and no - bod - y walks a step be - hind and there's

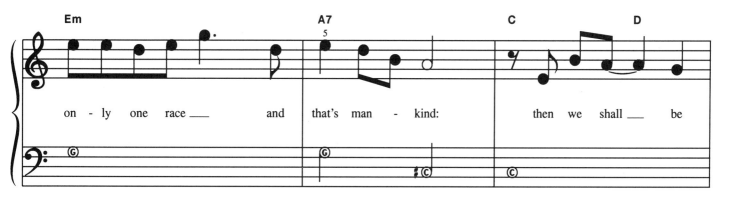

on - ly one race ___ and that's man - kind: then we shall ___ be

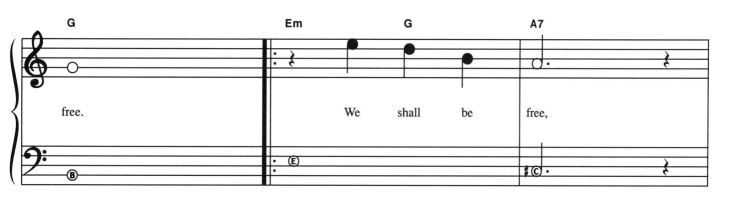

free. We shall be free,

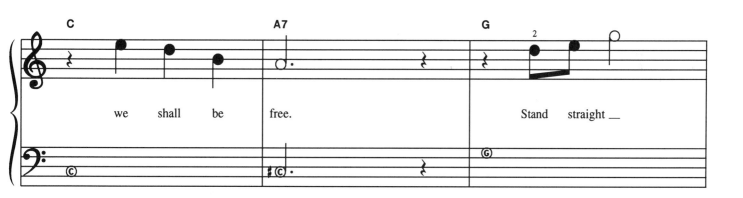

we shall be free. Stand straight ___

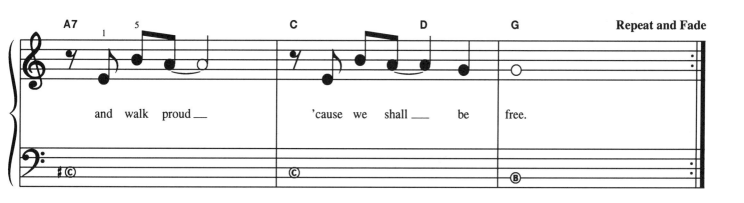

Repeat and Fade

and walk proud ___ 'cause we shall ___ be free.

YOUR CHEATIN' HEART

Words and Music by
HANK WILLIAMS

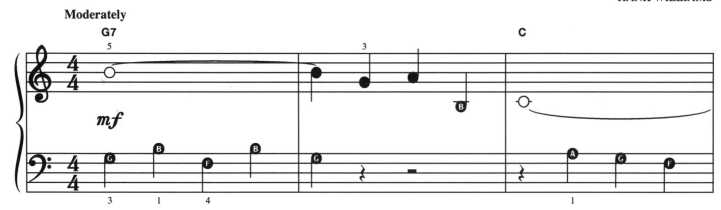

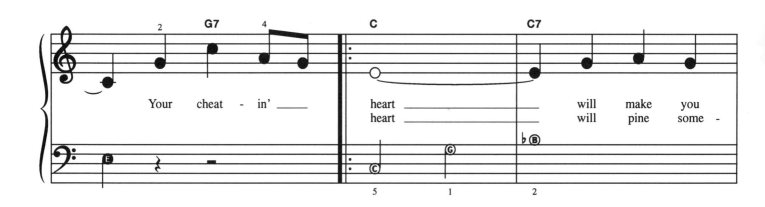

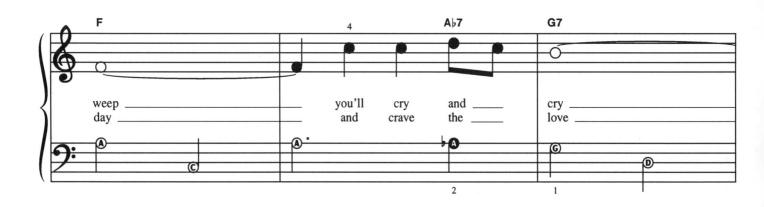

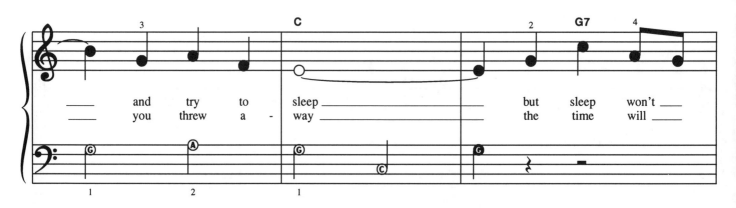

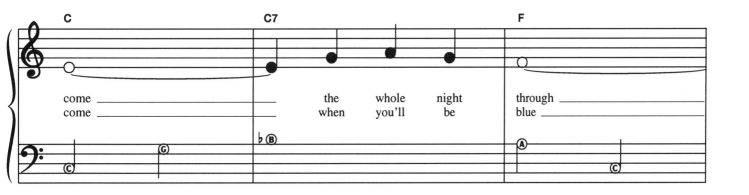

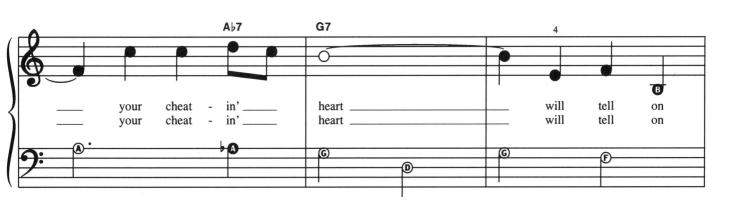

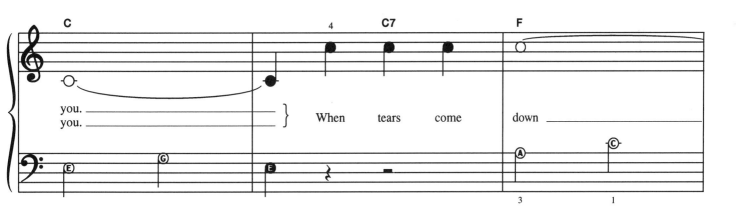

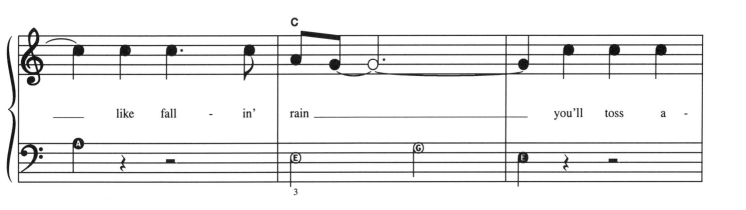

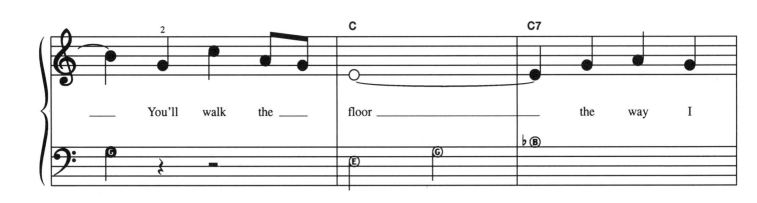

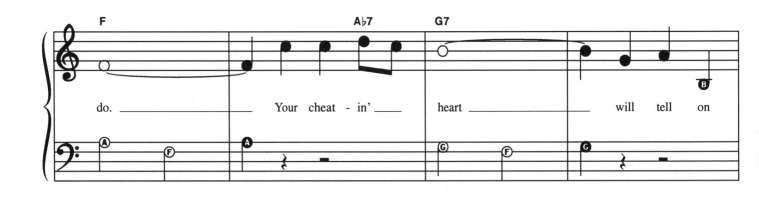

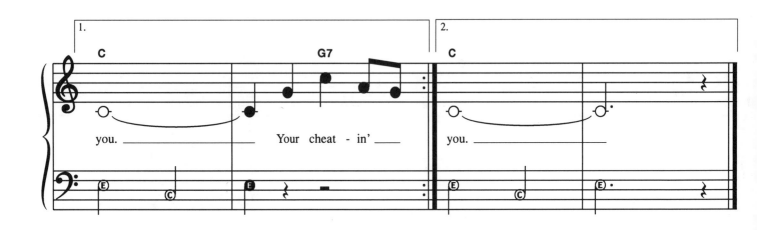

EASY ADULT Piano

These books, for all acoustic and electronic pianos, feature professional piano arrangements designed for amateur adult pianists. They're easy to read and easy to play so even beginners can play their favorite songs quickly, easily, and well. Chord symbols are included for use with the automatic chord feature found on many portable keyboards and electronic keyboards. Basic directions help the player get started.

EASY ADULT PIANO BEGINNER'S COURSE
160 pages of step-by-step piano instruction that begins in easy A-B-C notation in the treble clef and easy play in the bass clef. Over 40 songs, including: Greensleeves • Scarborough Fair • The Entertainer • Mozart's Theme. Professionally arranged to make adult beginners sound great and inspire them to continue to learn. A-B-C stickers included.
00001101 . . . .$14.95

PIANO IN THE DARK AND OTHER SOFT HITS
Arranged by Joe Raposo
15 songs: Don't You Know What The Night Can Do • Make Me Lose Control • Moonlighting • Piano In The Dark • On My Own and more.
00001490 . . . .$7.95

PIANO CLASSICS
Arranged by Joe Raposo
22 favorites, including Claire de Lune by Debussy • Fleur de Lis by Beethoven • Liebestraum by Liszt • Polonaise by Chopin • Romeo And Juliet by Tchaikovsky • Tales From The Vienna Woods by Strauss and more.
00001022 . . . .$7.95

CLASSIC LOVE SONGS
17 sentimental favorites, including: All The Things You Are • Endless Love • I Will Always Love You • Just The Way You Are • Save The Best For Last • Somewhere Out There • When I Fall In Love • A Whole New World • and more.
00243164 . . . .$7.95

COUNTRY HITS
20 songs, including: Achy Breaky Heart • Boot Scootin' Boogie • Chattahoochee • Forever And Ever, Amen • Friends In Low Places • Love Can Build A Bridge • No One Else On Earth • and more.
00243165 . . . .$7.95

AS TIME GOES BY
Arranged by Joe Raposo
15 songs, including: As Time Goes By • Embraceable You • How Long Has This Been Going On • Misty • The More I See You • Someone To Watch Over Me and more.
00001021 . . . .$7.95

FAVORITE STANDARDS FROM YESTERYEAR
18 songs, including: Blue Moon • Isn't It Romantic • Love Is A Many Splendored Thing • Mona Lisa • Moon River • Over The Rainbow and more.
00001615 . . . .$7.95

FROM A DISTANCE (AND OTHER EASY LISTENING FAVORITES)
14 favorites, including: After The Lovin' • Love Story (Where Do I Begin?) • We've Only Just Begun • You Light Up My Life • and more.
00001616 . . . .$7.95

GREAT MOVIE SONGS OF ALL TIME
16 songs, including Arthur's Theme (Best That You Can Do) • Chariots Of Fire • (Everything I Do) I Do It For You • Theme From Ice Castles (Through The Eyes Of Love) • Up Where We Belong • and more.
00001614 . . . .$7.95

CHRISTMAS AT THE PIANO
30 songs: Have Yourself A Merry Little Christmas • I'll Be Home For Christmas • Let It Snow! Let It Snow! Let It Snow! • Silver Bells • and more holiday favorites.
00001491 . . . .$7.95

FRIENDS AND LOVERS
Arranged by Joe Raposo
14 songs, featuring: Both To Each Other • Evergreen • Killing Me Softly With His Song • Saving All My Love For You • We've Got Tonight • You've Lost That Loving Feeling and more.
00001023 . . . .$7.95

BROADWAY FAVORITES
20 favorite songs, including: Climb Ev'ry Mountain • Getting To Know You • I Dreamed A Dream • Let Me Entertain You • Memory • and more.
00243162 . . .$8.95

JAZZ CLASSICS
20 songs, including: April In Paris • Don't Get Around Much Anymore • How High The Moon • It Don't Mean A Thing (If It Ain't Got That Swing) • When I Fall In Love • and more.
00243163 . . . .$7.95

THE PHANTOM OF THE OPERA
9 songs from the Broadway smash, including: All I Ask Of You • Angel Of Music • The Phantom Of The Opera • The Music Of The Night • and more.
00001632 . . . .$12.95